Executive Compensation

Executive Compensation

Accounting and Economic Issues

Gary Giroux

BEP BUSINESS EXPERT PRESS

First published in 2015 by
Business Expert Press, LLC
222 East 46th Street, New York, NY 10017
www.businessexpertpress.com

ISBN-13: 978-1-60649-878-1 (paperback)
ISBN-13: 978-1-60649-879-8 (e-book)

Business Expert Press Financial Accounting and Auditing Collection

Collection ISSN: 2151-2795 (print)
Collection ISSN: 2151-2817 (electronic)

Cover and interior design by Exeter Premedia Services Private Ltd.,
Chennai, India

First edition: 2015

10 9 8 7 6 5 4 3 2 1

Printed in the United States of America.

Abstract

The chief executive officer (CEO) of a corporation and his or her executive team are responsible for the management of the business and its continued operating and financial success. The CEO and executive team are almost always highly compensated and the relative total compensation has mushroomed over time. Most of the compensation now is designed to be performance-based, but leading to charges that executives have incentives to manipulate corporate earnings and stock price in the short-term for their own self interests. The compensation at some companies became so egregious (Enron and other tech-bubble failures or Citigroup and other banks during the subprime meltdown) that compensation again became a major public policy issue subject to federal regulation. (Popular outrage and calls for government action against well-paid CEOs has been common at least since the 1930s.)

Questions about this vital topic abound: Are executives paid what they are worth? Are compensation incentive structures effective in motivating executives to promote the interests of investors, employees, customers and other stakeholders? Do current accounting and reporting standards provide adequate information on the effectiveness of compensation? Does economic theory and empirical evidence provide the appropriate framework for evaluating compensation decisions? Would a historical analysis provide a useful perspective for current and future requirements?

This book focuses on the major topics related to executive compensation—present, past and future. First is understanding what executive compensation is, including composition and objectives of pay contracts. Then, how do specific compensation agreements affect corporate behavior and performance? Third, what are the major components, including how and what are accounted for and disclosed? How is compensation, especially executive compensation accounted for—that is, what are the calculations and journal entries required? Fourth, what does historical analysis tell us about the topic, especially how contractual decisions have been made and what has worked. Part of the historical analysis is regulation, which has a long, complex history—usually fueled by public outrage, regulation often resulted in unintended consequences. As separate chapter focuses on academic research associated with U.S. firm, which has studied the issues for decades. International national developments also are important, including both accounting issues and academic research. Finally, what is in store for the future—both expected compensation agreements and what the compensation incentives suggest for future corporate decisions on operations and accounting manipulation.

Three key points are emphasized. First is the role of accounting and disclosure in the process. Transparency has increased over time and compensation components seemingly are accounted for more effectively. Research analysis based on these disclosures suggests certain overall results about the composition and reasonableness of executive pay. Second is the importance of a historic/chronological perspective. The business culture and institutional framework have changed dramatically since the 1930s, with important ramifications. The role of the Securities and Exchange Commission (SEC) has been important beginning in the 1930s and the Financial Accounting Standards Board (FASB) for the last 40 years. Types and amounts of executive pay have bounced up and down based on tax laws and regulatory changes—often because of unintended causes, as executives found new ways to be paid more. The Timeline at the end of the book is quite useful putting this changing framework in perspective. Third is the importance of theory (especially economic) and empirical findings that help explain what is happening. Researchers have been investigating compensation worldwide and their findings are often different from the popular press. Overall, for example, compensation appears to be less egregious than previously thought. Finally, executive compensation continues to be the leading incentive structure driving short-term financial focus and potential accounting manipulation.

This short book can be used as a supplement in introductory financial accounting courses (especially at the intermediate level), accounting theory, as well as accounting- and finance-related MBA courses. Non-accounting business courses could include managing human resources, business and managerial finance, corporate governance, and labor economics. In addition, it can be useful for accounting and finance professionals wanting exposure to the details and incentive structures of this complex topic, including transparency (especially financial disclosure) issues and the relationship of compensation to accounting risks. Executives, board members and other looking to expand their knowledge of compensation issues and corporate governance should find the book useful. Compensation issues are important to public policy and those in government or interested in public policy also should find this book helpful.

Keywords

agency theory, compensation accounting, economic theory, executive compensation, proxy statement and 10-k disclosure, stock options/stock-based compensation

Contents

CHAPTER 1

Introduction to Executive Compensation

Too often, executive compensation in the U.S. is ridiculously out of line with performance.

—Warren Buffet

The chief executive officer (CEO) of a corporation and his or her management team are responsible for the operations of the business and its continued financial success. The CEO and executive team are almost always highly paid and their relative total compensation has mushroomed over time. Most of the compensation is now designed to be performance based because of the charges that executives manipulate their earnings and stock price for their own self-interest. The compensation at some companies became so egregious (Enron and other tech-bubble failures or Citigroup and other banks during the subprime meltdown) that it again became a major public policy issue subject to federal regulation. Popular outrage and calls for government action against well-paid CEOs have been common at least since the 1930s.

Questions about this vital topic abound: Are executives paid more than they are worth? Are compensation incentive structures effective in motivating executives to promote the interests of investors, employees, customers, and other stakeholders? Do current accounting and reporting standards provide adequate information on the effectiveness of compensation? Does economic theory and empirical evidence provide the appropriate framework for evaluating compensation decisions? Would a historical analysis provide a useful perspective for current and future requirements?

This book focuses on the major topics related to executive compensation—present, past, and future. (1) What is executive compensation, including composition and objectives of pay contracts? (2) How do specific compensation agreements affect corporate behavior and performance? (3) What are the major components, including how and what are accounted for and disclosed? (4) What does historical analysis tells us about the topic, especially how contractual decisions have been made and what has worked? Part of the historical analysis is regulation, which has a long, complex history—usually fueled by public outrage. Regulation often resulted in unintended consequences. Chapter 5 focuses on academic research, which studied the issues for decades, and has a set of theories, models, and empirical tests. Chapter 6 analyzes international comparisons, because U.S. results differed from those of other countries. Finally, what is in store for the future—both expected compensation agreements and what the compensation incentives suggest for future corporate decisions on operations and accounting manipulation.

Three key points are emphasized. First is the role of accounting and disclosure in the process. Transparency has increased over time and compensation components seemingly are accounted for more effectively. Research analysis based on these disclosures suggests certain overall results about the composition and reasonableness of executive pay, although alternative perspectives have different interpretations. Second is the importance of a historical (or chronological) perspective. Business cultures and institutional frameworks have changed dramatically since the 1930s, with important ramifications. The role of the Securities and Exchange Commission (SEC) has been important since the 1930s and the Financial Accounting Standards Board (FASB) for the last 40 years. Types and amounts of executive pay have bounced up and down based partly on tax laws and regulatory changes—often because of unintended causes, as executives found new ways to be paid more. The timeline at the end of the book is quite useful putting this changing framework in perspective. Third is the importance of theory (especially economic) and empirical findings that help explain what is happening. Researchers have been investigating compensation worldwide and their findings are often different from those of the popular press. Overall, for example, compensation may be less egregious than previously thought. Finally, executive compensation continues to be the leading incentive structure driving a short-term financial focus and potential accounting manipulation by public corporations.

What is Executive Compensation?

The major corporate executives are usually considered the CEO and the CEO's top lieutenants, including the chief financial officer (CFO), president, and chief operating officer (COO). However, according to Ellig, executives can be defined by "salary, job grade, key position, job title, reporting relationship or a combination."[1] So, a bit of care must be taken in the analysis. The SEC requires considerable disclosure for the CEO, CFO, and other executives with the highest compensation—called the "named executive officers" (NEOs). The SEC definition will be the one used most of the time.

The SEC Proxy Statement is the place to turn to define executive compensation. The summary compensation table has the following categories for the most recent three years: salary, bonus, stock awards, options awards, nonequity incentive plan compensation, change in pension value plus deferred compensation, and all other compensation. The sum of these seven columns is the total compensation. Summary compensation table for Microsoft, 2013 is a reasonable place to start an analysis, although there are many more disclosures and complex reporting. The details (and there are many) are described in the SEC's S-K Regulations.[2]

Table 1.1 shows the summary executive compensation of Microsoft for fiscal year 2013. (A more complete disclosure of Microsoft's Proxy Statement information on executive compensation is presented and analyzed in Appendix 1.) Although CEO at the time Steve Ballmer (a multibillionaire with wealth estimated at $20.7 billion, number 32 on the *Forbes* 400 list) made less than $1.3 million, other senior executives were quite well paid. The remaining five received huge stock awards up to $7.5 million and cash bonuses up to over $2 million.

The base salary is the cash compensation figure the executive expects to receive no matter what. Basic pension benefits and perquisites also usually are paid under all circumstances. Most of the remaining components are "performance-based," meaning that the amounts presumably will rise and fall as corporate performance changes, usually one or more measures of accounting earnings and stock performance as specified in the compensation contract. Specific terms can be complex and often require multiyear measurements and vesting periods. More coverage on this point in upcoming chapters.

Table 1.1 Summary compensation table for Microsoft, 2013

Name and Principal Position	Year	Salary ($)	Bonus ($)	Stock awards ($)	All other compensation ($)	Total ($)
Steven A. Ballmer: CEO and director	2013	697,500	550,000	N/A	13,718	1,261,218
	2012	685,000	620,000	N/A	13,128	1,318,128
	2011	682,500	682,500	N/A	11,915	1,376,915
Amy E. Hood: CFO	2013	365,954	457,443	6,626,019	11,153	7,460,569
Peter S. Klein: former CFO	2013	598,333	N/A	3,542,323	11,820	4,152,476
	2012	580,000	950,000	3,567,806	11,030	5,108,836
	2011	525,000	720,000	2,266,321	10,366	3,521,687
Kurt D. DelBene: president, Microsoft Office Division	2013	669,167	1,505,625	5,406,699	10,954	7,592,445
	2012	638,333	1,812,500	5,445,594	10,298	7,906,725
	2011	603,333	1,450,000	4,154,922	10,994	6,219,249
Satya Nadella: president, Server and Tools	2013	669,167	1,580,906	5,406,699	12,180	7,668,952
B. Kevin Turner: COO	2013	777,500	2,138,125	7,457,504	10,484	10,383,613
	2012	762,500	2,400,000	7,511,150	10,021	10,683,671
	2011	732,500	1,925,000	6,610,104	9,537	9,277,141

Paying Executives What They Are Worth

What could a CEO or any other executive actually be worth? Many of them are paid a lot, but not all. Steve Jobs, as CEO of Apple Computer and arguably one of the best CEOs of all time, was often paid a dollar a year. Conveniently, he was a billionaire, but certainly not overpaid most years. Warren Buffett, head of Berkshire Hathaway, had a long-time annual salary of $100,000 a year (also a billionaire and one of the richest men in the world).

On the other hand, many executives received unbelievable sums. Larry Ellison, CEO of Oracle (another billionaire), received a pay package of $96.2 million in 2012 (up 24 percent from 2011), even though total returns for Oracle fell 22 percent.[3] A pay survey by GMI ratings indicated that Mark Zuckerberg, CEO and founder of Facebook, received $2.3 billion in compensation thanks to exercised options and Richard Kinder of Kinder Morgan, $1.1 billion. Billion dollar pay is rare and the average executive pay is much lower. On the other hand, pay increases tend to be generous for executives, while raises for average workers typically stingy. The median pay increase was 8.5 percent across over 2,200 North American CEOs, 19.7 percent for the S&P 500.[4]

Equal public outrage involves the exit packages of CEOs fired for mediocre performance or worse. The record for outrageous termination pay is still held by former Disney CEO Michael Eisner, receiving a $550 million exit package after being canned in 1997. Eisner had plenty of competition including Michael Ovitz's severance, also from Disney in 1995 (ironically fired by Eisner—Disney apparently had plenty of funds to pay for bad management), at $130 million; Richard Grasso forced out from the New York Stock Exchange (NYSE) presidency after receiving $140 million (the NYSE was a nonprofit organization at the time); Robert Nardelli with an exit package from Home Depot of $210 million, Hewlett-Packard's Carly Fiorina ($21 million); and numerous others. Enron executives received some $500 million in total pay in the second half of the 1990s, enough to encourage ongoing deceit through the end of that decade.

A number of CEOs were paid gigantic salaries and likely well worth it. Robert Goizueta, long-time CEO of Coca-Cola, became the first nonowner of a public company to receive more than a billion dollars in total compensation over his career (1981 to 1997). Jack Welch of General Electric (GE) was well compensated over a long career at GE, including 20 years as chairman and CEO (1981 to 2001). The market value of GE increased over 30 times while he was CEO (from $14 billion to more than $400 billion), although he earned the epithet *Neutron Jack* for terminating thousands of employees. His retirement/severance package was later valued at $420 million, enough to tarnish his reputation—in part because parts of it were hidden (until disclosed during a nasty divorce). Other large retirement packages from major corporations included Lee Raymond of Exxon (2005, $321 million) and Louis Gerstner of IBM (2002, $189 million).

The Economics of Labor and Compensation

Executive pay has long been an important part of labor economics and economics in general. Labor is one of the factors of production (inputs), along with capital, land, and (in some models) entrepreneurship. Other factors such as natural resources, technology, infrastructure, or capital stocks can be considered separately or as parts of the major factors of production. Output is usually measured as finished goods. *Labor* in economic terms measures the work done by humans, including issues associated with the demand and supply of labor; skill levels; and impact on wages, incomes, and overall employment. In neoclassical economics, the demand and supply of labor markets determine prices (wage rates) and quantity (employment). Labor behaves differently from other production factors. If supply is greater than demand, the result is unemployment (a problem of public policy, not necessarily business). If demand is greater (overall or for specific skills), additional supply is not easily generated as wages rise. Labor markets within firms focus on how firms set up, maintain, and end employment relationships, while providing incentives to maintain efficiency and avoid employee shirking.

Executive compensation models in economics generally are based on an agency framework. Agency is a branch of law where a principal authorizes an agent to create legal contracts/relationships with third parties. This is a fiduciary relationship requiring the agent to be loyal to the principal. A corporation is a legal entity relying on human agents. Although based on legal terms, economic agency theory was developed by Jensen and Meckling in a 1976 paper. Underlying assumptions are that corporations (and other organizations) seek profit; principals and agents are rational; agents seek additional returns (rent seeking); principals are risk neutral but agents are risk adverse; and agency costs are major factors to consider in writing contracts. As in most economic models following neoclassical assumptions, the results are mathematically elegant but not especially realistic.[5]

During the Roaring Twenties, the very rich reached the pinnacle of wealth. As the Great Depression hit, Congressional hearings and various investigations discovered million-dollar salaries of a few at the top, tax cheats, and rampant fraud. An outraged public demanded action and federal regulators gathered compensation data of the top executives— which has continued to this day. With this growing database, economists could develop and test various hypotheses about compensation and its impact on firm behavior. Early studies were descriptive, such as John Baker's *Executive Salaries and Bonus Plans* published in 1938. New Deal legislation, high tax rates and World War II wage controls held executive compensation in check—a period called the *Great Compression*, which lasted into the 1980s.

In a pair of 1990 articles, Robert Jensen and Kevin Murphy laid out an economic argument for performance-based compensation based on an agency framework and a wealth of data.[6] The more influential article was published in *Harvard Business Review*, which claimed that CEOs were paid like bureaucrats without regard to actual corporate performance. Their empirical analysis showed that CEO compensation in the 1980s (adjusted for inflation) was actually less than that in the mid-1930s (during the middle of the Great Depression). Based on agency incentives, Jensen and Murphy claimed that CEO stock ownership was too low for efficient contracting based on *pay-performance sensitivity*. Their suggested solution was an increased use of stock options to properly align the interests of the CEOs with shareholders. This proved to be one of the rare cases where action followed academic research as corporations loaded options on CEOs as well as other executives and employees. The 1990s proved to be the main period of the Great Divergence as CEO pay exploded while average pay stalled.

Hundreds of academic papers followed, many using a Jensen–Murphy model of "efficient contracting," the agency concept related to optimal behavior. By aligning the incentives of CEOs with the interests of investors through performance-based pay (especially stock options), a competitive equilibrium maximizes the value of the firm. The primary alternative framework was "managerial power," stressing that gigantic pay packages were the result of CEOs effectively capturing the board of directors rather than competitive forces at work and the downsides of using options, the incentives to cheat because of the rewards, would not become obvious until the tech bust and the discovery of major frauds at Enron, WorldCom, and other large corporations.

Misguided Incentives and the Potential for Manipulation

While average executive compensation tended to be reasonable, the top compensation seemed outrageous to most observers (especially the public, media, and politicians). It was the publication of these outrageous salaries—the million-dollar salaries of the 1920s, the incredible retirement and termination packages of various CEOs in the post–World War II period, and the hundreds of millions paid in the 1990s to leaders of major corporations committing massive fraud—that resulted in regulation and attempts at reform.

The typical executive pay at corporations historically was a straight contract-based salary. At least from the beginning of the 20th century, various attempts have been made to provide additional pay incentives, from cash and stock bonuses, longer-term stock-based programs, stock purchase plans, retirement plans, and multiple perquisites. These often followed changes in taxes and other regulations. One interesting feature was that firms that used various bonuses and other plans paid these on top of previously competitive-based salaries, particularly obvious from compensation data from the 1920s and 1930s. According to Baker, the majority of large corporations paid bonuses of some type (64 percent) in the 1920s, but the base salaries of the salary-only and salary-plus-bonus firms was about the same while the total compensation of salary-plus-bonus firms was more than double of salary-only firms.[7]

The Congressional Pecora Commission hearings investigated the causes of the 1929 market crash and the business practices of the 1920s, especially banking and Wall Street. This included fraud cases such as Kruger and Toll and stock pyramiding at Insull's electric empire and other utility and railroad holding companies. Many illicit practices were uncovered, from insider trading to stock manipulation, but virtually all of them were considered legal at the time. The Securities Acts of the 1930s were designed to reform corporate and market behavior. A major focus was on disclosure, assuming that complete information to stockholders and other users would eliminate much of the abuse. Included in new requirements were annual reporting requirements on the compensation of CEOs and other top executives, which may have had a dampening effect on compensation, possibly for decades.

The post–World War II period saw economic growth and a rising stock market. Executives did not participate much in the bull market from the mid-1950s to mid-1960s, in part because of high tax rates. This was followed by a bear market and stagflation until the early 1980s. The Reagan revolution, lower tax rates, and an antiregulatory environment was a favorable climate for compensation. However, it was the call for stock options and performance-based compensation that propelled ethically-challenged CEOs and other executives to focus on the measurements that drove executive salaries, mainly quarterly earnings and stock prices. The result was massive manipulation rather than matching the long-term interests of investors. Accounting earnings, stock prices, financial manipulation, and executive salaries exploded upward together. Particularly, the period of the tech bubble (roughly 1995 to 2000) proved to be both a scam period as well as one of innovation and progress. A similar euphoric psychology happened with the mortgage bubble of the mid-2000s. Another house of cards, financial collapse and the government trying to salvage the economy and reform the system. With few exceptions, CEOs and other executives did quite well relying on compensation contracts that functioned well for executives even in periods of economic chaos. This included the subprime meltdown, Great Recession, and beyond.

Economic Modeling

The SEC demanded executive compensation disclosures since the mid-1930s and economists have analyzed the data ever since. Over the last 80 or so years that compensation data have been available, the economy, culture, government regulation, and perceived role of corporate pay have changed—as have the theories to explain the differences. Compensation was roughly flat for at least the first half of this period, only to explode, especially in the 1990s, thanks primarily to stock options. Economic research went along for the ride, introducing new theories (e.g., efficient contracting, managerial power) and new drivers to explain the changing results.

Most of the economic model building since the 1980s has been based on agency theory, basically meaning that the executives are the agents for the stockholders (the principals) and the two parties have specific theoretical characteristics that can be modeled and tested empirically. Several alternative explanations have been developed within the agency framework, including efficient contracting, managerial power, and perceived cost. The models used and their relative effectiveness in explaining pay types and size changed partly in response to new pay characteristics, with changing government regulation being a major factor. New regulations (and their impact on pay decisions) can be difficult to model and explain theoretically, but this has not stopped researchers from trying. Whether the reader agrees with the specific models specified, the empirical results continue to be interesting.

International Comparisons

Other countries have not been particularly forthcoming with disclosures necessary to analyze executive compensation in detail. Specific disclosure requirements for high-pay executives (particularly the CEO) did not begin until the 1990s, and even that was done only within a few countries. Before then, analysis was based on limited survey data and aggregate measures available. Therefore, a long-term perspective on Euro-pay and beyond is not readily available.

Accounting standards in foreign countries differ from U.S. standards (generally accepted accounting principles or GAAP). Most countries (and all analyzed here) adopted International Financial Reporting Standards (IFRS) by around 2009. Britain and Canada began reporting executive pay in the 1990s. By the mid-2000s, executive compensation for specific leaders was disclosed within the public companies of many developed countries. When compared to U.S. pay, foreign executives were paid much less (associated with the "U.S. pay premium"); however, a substantial proportion could be explained by firm size, various structural characteristics, and the relative riskiness of U.S. pay with its reliance on stock options.

What Is Ahead?

Various perspectives are presented in the next six chapters to capture the multiple complexities of the topic as simply as possible. From almost any point of view, the topic is complicated. Chapter 2 covers compensation basics, defining the fundamental components, examples of past and current pay (many outrageous), long-term trends since the 1930s, the special issues of terminations and retirements, and compensation strategy and planning. Chapter 3 reviews accounting for compensation in some detail, including calculations, journal entries, and disclosures. Chapter 4 reviews the historical record of executive compensation, mainly since the 1930s. Chapter 5 explains economic modeling and empirical testing, based primarily on agency theory. Most of the papers reviewed cover the last 25 years, the period when current pay practices and modern economic analysis were developed. Chapter 6 describes recent international comparisons: U.S. pay practices versus those of Europe, Canada, and other developed countries. U.S. pay has been consistently higher than that of foreign counterparts, but this is partly explainable by differences in pay practices, size, industry, relative risk, and structural differences—according to economists' claims. Chapter 7 is my attempt to predict the future of executive pay (I do not see pay declining anytime soon) and what this means for the future of business and the economy. Also included are timelines and a glossary of basic terms.

CHAPTER 2

Compensation Basics

How people are paid affects their behaviors at work, which affects an organization's success. For most employers, compensation is a major part of total cost, and often it is the single largest part of operating cost. These two factors together mean that well-designed compensation systems can help an organization achieve and sustain competitive advantage.

—Milkovich, Newman, and Gerhart

Executive pay is part of all compensation paid by corporations and many of the details are much the same. Consequently, this chapter includes compensation basics as well as the additional details associated with executives. Compensation represents wages or salaries paid to employees plus bonuses and other benefits. Cash compensation is mainly base salary but may also include bonuses and other incentive payments. Total compensation includes benefits such as health care and retirement plus other noncash compensation such as stock options. A formal definition is: "All forms of financial return and tangible services and benefits employees receive as part of an employment relationship."[1]

Compensation Components

Base pay is usually determined on some combination of the value of skills, education, experience, seniority, and on-the-job performance—the elements of human capital. Base pay is a fixed contractual amount that does not vary by performance. Across different industries and corporations exist many examples of alternative perspectives. For example, Milkovich, Newman, and Gerhart compare Walmart and Costco. They are competitors in discount retail and compete on low prices (especially Walmart subsidiary Sam's Club and Costco). Compensation for both is primarily base pay. As part of Walmart's low-cost strategy, entry-level workers were paid low (about $8.40 an hour, somewhat higher at Sam's Club in 2014) and the average cashier wage was $8.62. Costco paid more ($11 for entry-level workers and $15.54 for the average cashier). Presumably, Costco attempts to attract higher-quality workers and retain them longer. On average, Walmart had an annual employee turnover of 50 percent, while Costco's was 20 percent. Costco annual revenue per employee was over $500,000, more than double that of Walmart. However, Walmart is much bigger and both firms have been successful in terms of revenue, earnings, and stockholder returns.[2] Michael Duke, Walmart's chief executive officer (CEO), earned $19.3 million in 2012, about 800 times the average employee salaries. Craig Selinek, Costco's CEO, earned $4.8 million, 48 times Costco's median salary. CEO compensation to average pay is one comparison used to measure pay equity. In this case, Costco appears considerably more equitable.

Cash compensation can include cost-of-living adjustments (COLAs) and merit raises. COLAs became a bigger deal during periods of high inflation. The concept is to maintain a specific standard of living. During the 1970s and early 1980s, inflation became a problem and rose over 10 percent annually by the end of the 1970s (as measured by the consumer price index or CPI). Labor unions in particular demanded COLAs.

A technical distinction exists between wages and salaries in the United States. A salary is paid to employees exempt from the Fair Labor Standards Act (FLSA) such as professionals and managers and they do not receive overtime pay. Base pay is usually fixed and set at a monthly or annual rate. The *nonexempt* employees are covered by the FLSA, paid an hourly wage, covered by overtime pay and subject to reporting requirements of the FLSA.[3] Merit raises are given as increases in base pay and measured on performance. Pay raises usually follow promotions.

Certain professionals are paid all or in part on a commission basis, especially in sales, such as a real estate agent or a car salesperson. This is another form of performance-based pay and subject to unique incentives. The salesperson must sell to be paid and usually incentivized to focus on more expensive, higher-priced goods—a top-of-the-line Avalon versus a base-model Prius, for example. For the buyer, *caveat emptor* (let the buyer beware) may be particularly important.

Cash bonuses are usually paid annually as a lump-sum payment for some measure of performance, such as income or sales or some combination of performance measures. Bonuses can be determined on an individual basis, awarded to all employees at some level as a standard dollar amount, a percentage of annual salary, or some other basis. These have been common at major corporations for executives at least since the 1920s. Salary plus cash bonuses also are called total cash compensation.

Stock ownership (such as stock options or restricted stock) given to employees should improve corporate earnings performance. However, the performance link is disputed and the empirical evidence is weak. The alternative perspective is that giving stock to employees dilutes shareholder wealth with limited obvious benefits. The rationale for ownership was especially prevalent beginning in the 1990s and focused mainly on executives. Jensen and Murphy in a famous 1990 article argued that CEO compensation should be based on performance and claimed that, in fact, CEOs of the time were "paid like bureaucrats."[4]

Since the 1990s, stock options and executive total compensation exploded for several reasons. First, Congress reduced personal income tax rates; the top rate was 28 percent with the Tax Reform Act of 1986, substantially increasing executive's after-tax income. The Revenue Reconciliation Act of 1993 capped executive pay at $1 million for a corporate tax deduction, but exempted performance-based pay—with options being the prominent performance-based alternative. Finally, both accounting and tax rules favored options. Accounting rules (until 2006) did not require recorded granting options as a compensation expense as long as the exercise price was the market price on the grant date or higher. However, when the grants were exercised a corporate tax deduction was allowed. Thus, options were considered *free money* and huge amounts of options often handed out, especially in the new high-tech companies. As stock prices rose and a tech bubble created in the late 1990s, options became extremely lucrative.

An interesting example is the pay of Apple cofounder Steve Jobs. He returned to Apple in 1997 and received one dollar a year in total salary in 1998 and 1999. He formally became CEO in 2000 and accepted options for 10 million shares. Apple recorded no compensation expense, although options pricing models indicated that they were worth about a quarter-billion dollars. Larry Ellison at Oracle took a similar deal about the same time: no salary from 2000 to 2003, but options on 10 million shares. *The Wall Street Journal* valued Ellison's windfall at $1.3 billion.[5]

After the tech crash of 2000 to 2001, based on the Sarbanes-Oxley Act of 2002, various regulators attempted to reign in out-of-control executives. Options and other performance incentives were perceived to encourage CEOs and others to cheat, a major factor in the many fraud scandals of the period. The Financial Accounting Standards Board (FASB) changed the rules on option accounting, requiring firms to record a compensation expense based on Black-Scholes or other options-pricing models. Firms moved much of their equity-based compensation from options to stock grants (usually restricted stock), stock appreciation rights, phantom stock, and other stock-based schemes.

Employee benefits such as sick leave, overtime pay, health insurance, and retirement have been common in the post–World War II period, but diminishing over the last 30 or so years. They were particularly important early on because of high individual tax rates, while these benefits were not taxed (or taxed under more favorable terms). One reason salaries and benefits to employees declined was increased foreign competition as workers competed with lower-paid workers from China and other developing countries. The relative power of labor, especially labor unions, also fell. The cost of health care rose substantially and life expectancy increased, making it difficult for corporations to maintain health care and retirement benefits at the old levels.

Executives in the post–World War II period typically received all the benefits given to rank-and-file employees and then some; for example, additional insurance, country club memberships. At that time (especially in the booming 1950s), executive pay was relatively low (partly because tax rates were so high, most salary increases were taxed away). Consequently, nontaxed benefits and perquisites became viable replacements for higher cash compensation.

Major companies often granted pensions in the form of defined benefit plans that granted monthly annuity payments after retirement generally based on some definition of final salary and years of service. This resulted in substantial long-term obligations and complex calculations. Employers used 401k plans since enacted into law in 1978, and defined contribution plans that allow all employees to contribute to retirement savings (often matched by the employer) on a tax-deferred basis. Under defined contribution plans, the employers have no further obligation for employee retirement. It becomes the responsibility of the employee to obtain enough retirement savings.

During the 1990s, most defined benefit retirement plans of major corporations were fully funded, in large part because of the booming stock market (and partly because of accounting rules that delayed full recognition of certain pension obligations). This changed in the twenty-first century, for several reasons. The tech crash dropped the values of pension investment portfolios substantially. Then the FASB changed the accounting rules, requiring companies to recognize additional pension obligations as well as other postemployment benefits on their balance sheets. Pensions had to be valued on funded status, the fair value of pension (investment) assets less all pension obligations (if the net amount was positive the plan was overfunded and vice versa). Companies used overfunded pensions to downsize the workforce, using pension assets to fund severance pay. Companies provided additional unfunded supplemental pensions (supplemental executive retirement plans or SERPs) to executives. This increased pension obligations, increased underfunding based on funded status, and the reporting made it seem that the employees' pension plans were underfunded. The perception by many analysts is that corporate executives and the board of directors care much more about executives than employees.

Employees and particularly executives received other benefits and perquisites. The major category was health insurance, a benefit whose costs have risen much more rapidly than inflation. Other common benefits included life insurance, child care, education opportunities, corporate cars, and so on. Executives likely had more expensive perks like corporate jets, executive dining, or country club memberships.

Another way of viewing compensation is fixed versus variable. Fixed compensation categories are low-risk components and include base salary and most of the various benefits and perquisites. Variable components are of higher risk and include bonuses and most stock-based compensation. These are generally performance based. The proper mix of fixed versus variable should be important to provide the right incentives for executives and employees—what that right mix happens to be remains debatable.

Compensation Comparisons

What is the reasonable compensation for a CEO or other executives? What is required for proper motivation to meet corporate objectives? What is considered fair based on ethical principles? Executive compensation agreements are complex and the various elements are related to various theories of compensation, from efficient contracting to managerial power to pay politics and public policy. Actual contracts vary from near-zero compensation to billion-dollar payouts (usually when executives exercise options and stock), while executive performance runs from total failure to brilliant. Various comparisons can be made: average pay over time, compensation based on corporate size and compensation increases relative to market value growth or other performance measures, and CEO pay to that of the average worker.

Executive pay over the last 100 or so years is a major concern of Chapter 4. In summary, the 1920s was a period of relatively high compensation (which now becomes apparent only by adjusting for inflation). Revelations in the 1930s showed million-dollar salaries of a few CEOs (although these were outliers because the average CEO salary of major corporations at the time was below $100,000). Executive salaries fell during the Great Depression of the 1930s and generally stayed down until the 1980s. There are several explanations for this result, also reviewed in Chapter 4. The real explosion in executive pay came in the 1990s as stock options became the most significant source of pay (helped by a booming stock market). Unfortunately, stock options and other incentives seemed a major cause of the many corporate fraud cases at large corporations at this time and uncovered after the tech crash of the early twenty-first century. Executive compensation moderated somewhat after the bubbles burst (both tech and the later mortgage bubble), particularly because of the declining use of stock options.

During most of the post–World War II period, CEO pay compared to that of the average worker was relatively low and usually considered fair. In 1965, the average CEO made $807,000 including options, about 20 times that of the average worker (according to the *Washington Post*). However, that ratio jumped to 273-to-1 in 2012, with the average salary of the top 350 CEOs topping $14 million. This was actually down on an inflation-adjusted basis from 383-to-1 in 2000 when the average CEO made $19.9 million.[6] The American Federation of Labor-Congress of Industrial Organizations (AFL-CIO), America's largest union and not CEO friendly, reported similar results based on the CEOs of the S&P 500. The CEO-to-worker pay ratio was 354 to 1 in 2012, up from 42 to 1 in 1982. The average CEO was paid over $12 million, with $4.5 million of that in stock awards. The average worker made less than $20 an hour, while many CEOs made over $10,000 an hour.[7,8]

CEO pay based on performance (and the vast majority is) should be closely related to stock market results. However, a 2013 Economic Policy Institute report showed that CEO pay rose twice as much as the stock market. The average CEO in the top 350 publicly traded companies earned over $14 million in 2012, up 875 percent from 1978, more than double the increase in stock prices over the same 1978 to 2012 period.[9]

Termination and Retirement

Employees can resign or be terminated involuntarily, considered a dismissal (*getting fired*, usually for cause) or a layoff (usually during business downturns). Financial considerations include possible severance pay (such as unused vacation or sick leave and other cash payments), continuing health insurance, and retirement benefits. Retirement starts when employment stops, often when employees are eligible for pension benefits, Social Security, or both.

Executives typically have more termination protection and their contracts can include various types of cash payments and benefits. CEOs at major corporations can have gigantic exit packages if terminated involuntarily. This usually means a combination of poor corporate performance or disagreement with the board of directors. Some examples are particularly interesting. At the top of my list is Robert Nardelli, fired from Home Depot with an exit package of $210 million (and later tabbed as one of the "worst American CEOs of all time" by CNBC). This was on top of the $240 million he earned over his tenure as CEO. However, outsize exit packages were fairly common in the 1990s and early twenty-first century.

Nardelli quit General Electric in 2000 after he was passed over for CEO in favor of Jeffrey Immelt to replace the legendary Jack Welch (more on him momentarily). Nardelli bounced back as chairman and CEO of Home Depot in late 2000. He restructured the floundering company, using many of the GE techniques such as Six Sigma. Over the next four years, sales rose 80 percent and earnings more than doubled. Unfortunately, Home Depot's stock remained flat (down about 40 percent from its 1999 high), while competitor Lowe's doubled. Much of this restructuring was geared to reducing costs, a major reason for the great earnings performance—and his outsized compensation. However, these cost cuts also reduced customer service. At the top of the questionable list of cost cutting were replacing experienced but expensive full-time employees with inexperienced part timers. Home Depot fell further behind Lowe's as customers favored better customer service and shifted their purchases to Lowe's. Nardelli seemed more interested in his pay package than repairing the declining reputation of Home Depot. He was finally canned in January 2007 and the stock price rose 3 percent on the news—seemingly his biggest contribution to the company.

Michael Ovitz was a talent agent when hired in 1995 by pal and CEO Michael Eisner to be president of Disney. Arguments between the two started almost immediately, presumably over "creative differences" and Ovitz' role in the company. He was fired by Eisner early in 1997, taking with him a severance package of $38 million in cash and $131 million in stock. Shareholders sued Disney and Eisner for the outsized award—essentially big bucks to stop doing a lousy job—but lost in court. Michael Eisner had his own problems. He was chairman and CEO for over 20 years, during which the stock rose over 1,600 percent. Disney hit a rough patch beginning in the late 1990s and he had a nasty fight with Roy Disney (Walt's nephew) who resigned from the board. Eisner was out in 2005 after earning about a billion dollars, mainly in stock options.

Henry McKinney, a long-time CEO of pharmaceutical giant Pfizer got a 72 percent pay increase in 2005, although Pfizer was losing money and the stock price had dropped almost in half. He was gone in 2006, taking with him an $83 million pension. William McGuire of United Health Group received some $1.6 billion in options, extremely valuable because the options were issued on the days the stock price hit the annual low. He was investigated by the Internal Revenue Service (IRS) and Justice Department for stock backdating, forced out as CEO and paid back some $600 million in claw backs. CEO Stan O'Neal exited Merrill Lynch in the same quarter of 2007 Merrill lost $2.3 billion and paid fines related to the mortgage crisis. To ease the pain, his exit package was worth over $160 million.

Executives also retire, sometimes with a big pension, deferred compensation, and benefits package. Particularly at the corporate top, compensation contracts can be quite detailed and complex about these benefits (plus the true costs were often hidden from the public). Executives usually receive the pension benefits available to all employees, called *tax qualified* and often SERPs, essentially a deferred compensation agreement to pay additional cash. SERPs can be funded by the cash value of life insurance policies because of their tax-deferred characteristics.

Perhaps, the best example of an extraordinary retirement package was that of Jack Welch who retired from GE in 2001 after 20 years as chairman and CEO. Although wealthy at retirement (receiving something worth of $700 million on the job), he received an exit package worth an additional $417 million. Lee Raymond, former CEO of ExxonMobil, was a distant second with a retirement package worth $321 million in 2005. Several others had $100 million-plus deals.

Compensation Strategy

Compensation planning is part of the business strategy of the firm. By definition, strategy represents "the basic long-term goals and objectives of an enterprise, and the adoption of courses of action and the allocation of resources necessary for carrying out these goals."[10] Business strategy is established within the context of the firm's industry. Manufacturing differs from service industries. Economies of scale, for example, are more likely in manufacturing. Each industry has unique features. Firms usually focus on product differentiation or cost leadership; that is, innovation usually through research and development or becoming the low-cost producer. Each firm depends on its core competencies, such as customer service or efficient distribution. One basic strategic theory is *AMO theory*, where performance is based on ability, motivation, and opportunity.[11]

Each firm has its own pay structure, the set of pay rate differentials for the various jobs from systems engineers to janitors, based on specific criteria such as education, experience, or seniority. Part of the pay scheme is based on hierarchical structures within a specific job category. A major defense contractor such as Lockheed Martin may have half a dozen levels of engineers including trainees to senior engineers or chief engineers. Levels of work may vary from associates to professionals to executives, with various categories and titles in between. Included in the pay strategy is compensation to the CEO, other executives, and board members. These can vary from company to company even in the same industry.

CEO succession should be considered in the strategy, both when the current CEO should retire and grooming one or more executives as possible replacements. GE works hard at both. When Jack Welch retired in 2001 after 20 years as CEO (five former GE CEOs served longer than a dozen years), over 20 possible internal replacements were considered, included Jeff Immelt, the previously discussed Nardelli, and Jim McNerney (like Nardelli he left, to become head of 3M and is now CEO of Boeing). Immelt has been on the job as CEO ever since and closing in on 15 years. Presumably, Immelt (58 in 2014) will retire in the next few years, and the replacement process will be repeated. According to *The Wall Street Journal*, GE has several leading internal candidates ranging in age from 40 (Lorenzo Simonelli) to 57 years (Vice Chairman John Rice).[12]

CHAPTER 3

Accounting for Executive Pay

The salary of the chief executive of a large corporation is not a market award for achievement. It is frequently in the nature of a warm personal gesture by the individual to himself.

— John Kenneth Galbraith

Accounting and disclosure issues have been central to executive compensation practices and public policy since the formation of the Securities and Exchange Commission (SEC) and the establishment of generally accepted accounting principles (GAAP), beginning in the 1930s.[1] Most payroll accounting practices involving cash originated early and have changed only modestly since then. More complex rules, such as stock options and retirement benefits, proved difficult to formulate and changed substantially over time. Most of these issues get complicated and the coverage below will keep to the fundamentals.

This chapter reviews current accounting procedures and issues, including basic calculation, journal entries, and disclosures required by GAAP. Accounting issues start with basic payroll entries; most executive compensation procedures follow the same rules as all other employees: periodic wages, payments to governments for taxes owed, retirement and stock benefits available to all employees, and so on. Stock-based compensation plans are next up, including options, restricted stock, and stock appreciation rights (SARs). Each has its own characteristics, accounting issues, benefits, and drawbacks. The other complex category is pensions and other retirement benefits paid to both employees and executives. Specific calculations and journal entries using the fictional Gotrocks Corporation will be presented as separate exhibits. Executive compensation disclosures (from the 2013 Proxy Statement) and stock-based compensation (from the 2013 10-K) note are presented for Microsoft in Appendixes 1 and 2, respectively. Because Microsoft does not have a defined benefit plan nor an other post-employment benefits (OPEB) note, 10-K disclosures and analysis are presented for pharmaceutical giant Pfizer (which has both) for 2012 in Appendix 3.

The Financial Accounting Standards Board (FASB) codified GAAP in 2009. Prior to that, specific pronouncement on new or revised standards was presented numerically, such as Statement of Financial Accounting Standards (SFAS) 123R, which revised stock option accounting and SFAS 158 revising pension and OPEB. All of the active accounting standards became part of the Codification, which are listed by topics. For example, expenses are under 700, including compensation-general (710), compensation-nonretirement postemployment benefits (712), compensation-retirement benefits (715), and compensation-stock compensation (718).

Payroll Accounting

Employers pay employee salaries periodically, perhaps weekly, monthly, or bimonthly. The most difficult part from an accounting point of view is meeting the tax requirements and other deductions. The employer pays the net salaries to the employees in cash (most often in the form of direct deposit or check) and creates liabilities that are paid periodically throughout the year. The basic entries have not changed much since the start of GAAP and there are few if any controversial issues. Basic (simplified) payroll calculations and journals entries are presented in Exhibit 3.1. Accruals have to be made at the end of the fiscal year for compensation earned but not paid by the end of the year.

Exhibit 3.1 Payroll Accounting

Assume Gotrocks Corp. pays employees at a total rate of $140,000 monthly. The basic journal entry is:

Salaries expense	140,000	
Salaries payable		140,000

Other common pay categories include overtime, commission, bonuses, and various compensated absences such as vacation pay. In addition, federal law requires payroll and income taxes, and both federal and state laws require unemployment taxes. Employees and employers must each pay Social Security tax of 6.2 percent of gross salaries (up to $117,000 in 2014) and Medicare tax of 1.45 percent on all wages.[2] Federal unemployment insurance is paid by employers, usually at 0.8 percent plus state unemployment tax around 5.4 percent. These costs are paid for all employees, including executives.

The expanded entry to record the employees' monthly payroll might be:

Salaries expense	140,000
FICA taxes payable	10,786.50
Federal income taxes payable	14,000
Health insurance payable	9,800
Salaries payable	105,413.50

FICA, *Federal Insurance Contributions Act.*

In addition, the employer would have these additional liabilities and expenses:

Payroll tax expenses	29,266.50
FICA taxes payable	10,786.50
Federal unemployment taxes	1,120
State unemployment taxes	7,560
Health insurance payable	9,800

FICA, *Federal Insurance Contributions Act.*

These additional costs raise the compensation costs to almost $30,000, over 20 percent. This does not include additional costs for pensions, stock options, and other benefits to employees and executives. FICA stands for Federal Insurance Contributions Act, which requires both Social Security and Medicare taxes, which total 7.65 percent (6.2% + 1.45%) on both employees and employers ($140,000 × 7.65% = $10,786.50). Federal income tax is assumed to be 10 percent of the gross salaries ($140,000 × 10% = $14,000) and health insurance 7 percent ($140,000 × 7% = $9,800) on both employees and employers. Federal and state unemployment taxes are assumed to be

0.8 percent and 5.4 percent, respectively ($140,000 × 0.8% = $1,120; $140,000 × 5.4% = $7,560).

An additional accounting issue is compensation absences, payments for vacation, sick leave, holidays, and so on. Expenses have to be estimated for those charges that have been earned but not yet paid by the end of the fiscal year. For example, assume that most vacations are taken in the summer. However, the vacation time is related in part to the previous fiscal year. Assuming the estimate of vacation time at year-end was $850, the following accrual would be recorded:

Salaries expense	850
Vacation wages payable	850

Other year-end accruals are made if the fiscal year-end falls between pay periods. For example, assume that employees are paid weekly (on Friday) and the fiscal year-end is Wednesday. If the weekly pay totals $5,000, three-fifth of that ($3,000) is accrued for the current year on Wednesday (simplified), as follows:

Salaries expense	3,000
Salaries payable	3,000

On Friday, which is in the next year, the entry is:

Salaries expense	2,000
Salaries payable	3,000
Cash	5,000

Share-based Compensation

Executives and employees are often paid some form of ownership interest using stock options, restricted stock or SARs, and other mechanisms. All of them have unique accounting features and issues. In addition, employees can be granted the right to purchase corporate stock, usually at a reduced rate relative to the market value. Typical journal entries associated with share-based compensation are summarized in Exhibit 3.2.

Exhibit 3.2 Share-based Compensation Entries

Basic Stock Options

On January 1, 2013, Gotrocks' board authorized 10,000 stock options to the CEO. The closing stock price on that date (grant date) was $20 per share, which became the exercise (strike) price. The options vest in two years (becoming exercisable on January 1, 2015) and expire on December 31, 2015. Based on SFAS No. 123R, the options have a compensation value based on a pricing model such as Black Scholes. The calculated value is $8 per share or $80,000 based on Black Scholes. A memorandum entry is made on the grant date (January 1, 2013) and the $80,000 compensated value is accrued over the two-year vesting period, that is, $40,000 each year. The adjusting entry at December 31, 2013, is:

Compensation expense	40,000
Paid-in capital-stock options	40,000

A similar entry is made at the end of 2014.[3]

On the vesting date (January 1, 2015) the stock price is $35 and the CEO exercises the 10,000 options on that date. She would pay $200,000 to the company for the stock (10,000 shares times $20 per share), the strike price. The journal entry for this transaction on January 1, 2015, is:

Cash	200,000
Paid-in capital-stock options	80,000
Common stock (no par)	280,000

If instead the stock price drops to $15 and the options are not exercised, they would expire on December 31, 2015. That entry would be:

Paid-in capital-stock options	80,000
Paid-in capital-expired options	80,000

Note disclosure would be made for these transactions. The December 31, 2013, disclosures would include:

	Shares	Exercise price
Outstanding stock options, January 1, 2013	0	
Granted during 2013	$10,000	$20
Exercised during 2013	0	
Forfeited during 2013	0	
Outstanding at December 31, 2013	$10,000	$20
Options exercisable during 2013	0	
Weighted-average fair value of options granted during 2013	$8	
Compensation expense for stock options during 2013	$40,000	

The note disclosure also would include a description of the option plans and the models used to value the options.

Performance-based Options

Assume the same basic information for Gotrocks as above. The CEO is given 10,000 options on January 1, which vest in two years and are valued at $8 a share. She will be awarded an additional 6,000 options if the net income for fiscal year 2014 is greater than $20 million and an additional 4,000 options if the net income is over $25 million (potentially 20,000 options). The option value to be accrued is based on the expected net income in 2014. At the end of 2013, the projected net income for 2014 is $22 million, and the CEO is expected to receive the 10,000 base options plus 6,000 for meeting the over $20 million criterion. The December 31, 2013, entry would be:

Compensation expense	64,000	
Paid-in capital-stock options		64,000

The calculation is $8 times 16,000 options that equals $128,000 divided by two, $64,000, to obtain the first year's compensation from options.

The actual net income for 2014 was $26 million, meaning that the CEO was awarded 20,000 options for net income over $25 million. The December 31, 2014, entry would be:

Compensation expense	96,000
Paid-in capital-stock options	96,000

The calculation is $8 times 20,000 options that equals $160,000 less $64,000 accrued for 2013, $96,000.

On the vesting date (January 1, 2015) the stock price is $35 and the CEO exercises the 20,000 options on that date. She would pay $400,000 to the company for the stock (20,000 shares times $20 per share), the strike price. The journal entry for this transaction on January 1, 2015, is:

Cash	400,000
Paid-in capital-stock options	160,000
Common stock (no par)	560,000

Note that disclosure would include a table similar to the one above, except that it would show 20,000 options granted and compensation expense for 2013 of $64,000. In addition, the performance-based criteria for these options would be described.

Restricted Stock

Gotrocks awards restricted stock of 2,000 restricted shares to the CEO on January 1, 2013, which will vest in two years, on January 1, 2015. Because the ending stock price on the grant date is $20, the restricted shares are valued at $40,000, which would be recognized as a compensation expense of the two years. The December 31, 2013, journal entry recorded half of the cost as follows:

Compensation expense	20,000
Paid-in capital-restricted stock	20,000

A similar entry would be made on December 31, 2014.

On January 1, 2015, the restricted shares vested and were recorded as common stock:

Paid in capital-restricted stock	40,000
Common stock (no par)	40,000

Note that accounting for restricted stock is somewhat easier relative to stock options.

Stock Appreciation Rights

On January 1, 2013, the Gotrocks board approved an award of 5,000 SARs to the CEO, each of which will pay a cash amount equal to the market value of the stock above $25 a share in two years, by January 1, 2015. The SARs expire on December 31, 2015. Compensation expense will be based on the expected settlement amount. On December 31, 2013, it was forecast that Gotrocks' shares will be valued at $29, resulting in an expected SAR award of $4 a share ($29 − $25 = $4). The total value of the SARs was estimated at $20,000 ($4 per share times 5,000 shares). Half of this amount was an expense of the current year, using the following entry:

Compensation expense	10,000
Share-based compensation payable	10,000

At December 31, 2014, Gotrocks shares were valued at $35. The SAR value to be recorded was $50,000 ($10 per share above $25 times 5,000 SARs) less $10,000 accrued the previous year. The entry was recorded as:

Compensation expense	40,000
Share-based compensation payable	40,000

The CEO SARs vested on January 1, 2015, and she received the cash payment on that date.

Share-based compensation payable	50,000
Cash	50,000

Stock Options

Options allow the holder to purchase stock at a set price (the exercise price), usually the market closing price on the issue date of the options (grant date). Options became common in the 1990s at a time when they did not have to be expensed (if the exercise price was the closing price of the stock at the grant date); that is, the options were considered to have *an intrinsic value* of zero and no compensation expense was recorded. This did not change until 2006, with the introduction of SFAS No. 123R, *Accounting for Stock-based Compensation*; SFAS 123R required options to be valued using an options pricing model such as Black Scholes. The Black Scholes model was developed by Fischer Black and Myron Scholes in 1973, allowing options to be priced based on market information. The formula requires five inputs: current stock price, selling (strike) price, time to maturity, risk-free rate of return, and volatility of stock returns. All are observable except volatility, which must be estimated. Traders used this and similar formulas to price options and options trading exploded, as did new hedging and speculating instruments.[4]

Options were used by major corporations even before they could be adequately priced, especially during periods when they had favorable tax treatment. By 1961, 68 percent of New York Stock Exchange firms had option plans, largely because of favorable tax treatment.[5] Prior to SFAS No. 123, options were valued for accounting purposes at intrinsic value, which was zero if the exercise price was set at the closing market value at the grant date or later. The major driving forces were tax rules and tax rates (which changed often) and related regulations, rather than option pricing rules.

From the perspective of the holder, options have real advantages, because they represent one-directional payment—the holder participates in the gains over the exercise price and will exercise those options at some point. However, unlike stockholders, the options holder shares none of the losses. If the stock price drops below the exercise price, the *underwater* options are not exercised—no money is lost by the holder. From the company perspective, options have real costs (even before they were required to be treated as compensation expense). The options are dilutive; that is, they increase the number of shares outstanding (*dilution*). When calculating diluted earnings per share (EPS), EPS decreases. If, for example, options increase shares by 10 percent, net income has to increase 10 percent to maintain the same EPS. Many large corporations issued millions of options, especially high-tech companies, and many had outstanding options greater than 10 percent of shares outstanding such as Hewlett-Packard, IBM, and Intel.[6]

Basic options (which are time based) vest only if the employee stays with the company during the vesting period. With performance-based options, vesting depends on meeting specific performance criteria. Performance criteria could include level of sales, amount of net income, or other measures. This should encourage employees to work harder to meet these measures. The downside is the incentive to cheat to meet the criteria, a common result in the 1990s when options became widespread as did manipulation and fraud—including Enron and WorldCom.

Cash has to be paid by the recipient to the company when options are exercised for the strike price (also called exercise price), plus the capital gains on the options are taxed as capital gains. Consequently, the stock received is often sold by the recipient at the same time. This was a disadvantage compared to other equity-based compensation.

The primary problem with options was the perceived continuing need to cheat when accounting performance was not considered adequate. Potential compensation associated with options at many companies could be gigantic. Because companies did not have to record a compensation expense (before SFAS No. 123R became effective in 2006), massive options were often awarded and the potential payout could be huge— but only if the stock price kept climbing. Financial analysts focused on quarterly earnings and corporations were expected to *meet or beat* the consensus forecasts. If not, the stock price could be hammered. Consequently, a mad hustle for higher earnings could take place at the end of each quarter. Although this practice was widespread, the best evidence came from the books, hearings, criminal proceedings, and other analyses associated with Enron and other specific frauds. Enron was experienced at sophisticated deception and, as meeting expectations became more difficult, fraud. Techniques included using market value to restate asset pricing and recording gains (especially using *mark to model* to generate virtually any value the higher-ups wanted), deceptive energy trading gains and losses, and amazing abuse of special purpose entities to generate any level of gains as needed.[7]

The fraud and other abuses were eventually discovered, typically resulting in corporate bankruptcy and serious jail time for the perpetrators, certainly true of Enron, WorldCom, and many others. Options became less important in the twenty-first century as boards of directors, legislators, pundits, and academics were convinced that other forms of equity compensation would be more effective, such as restricted stock.

Restricted Stock

An ownership alternative to options is restricted stock, shares of the company stock that vest sometime in the future, based only on time or specific performance criteria. Once the stock vests, the employee has the right to obtain full ownership to the shares. The value of restricted stock goes up and down, and holders feel the pain if the stock price goes down (in other words, just like any other stockholder). One of the advantages when exercised is that no cash has to be paid out to acquire the shares (although tax has already been paid). Restricted stock also is less risky. The market prices of most large corporations hold their value over time. Options, on the other hand, are a much riskier bet, that stock prices will rise in the future. If so, the holder potentially makes a killing; if not, nothing.

Restricted stock has been more common in the twenty-first century, particularly after SFAS 123R became effective. From 2004 to 2010, restricted stock holdings for S&P 500 executives increased 88 percent.[8] Microsoft, for example, shifted from options to restricted stock in 2004 and options outstanding soon fell substantially (and stood at only four million at the end of the 2013 fiscal year). Of course, Microsoft leaders Bill Gates and Steve Ballmer held millions of shares and did not need additional options to be multibillionaires.

SARs and Phantom Stock

Stock appreciation rights (SARs) are cash or stock bonuses based on the appreciation of the company's stock over a specific time period. The employee usually has flexibility as to when to exercise the SARs. Unlike stock options, the employee does not have to buy the shares when exercised; however, the SAR payouts are treated as ordinary income for tax purposes. SAR cash payments represent equity-based compensation that does not dilute outstanding shares, which can make them especially useful to closely held and family-owned companies that want to maintain ownership control. As with options and restricted stock, SARs can be time or performance based.

Phantom stock is similar to SARs and promises a cash (or sometimes stock) payment at a future date based on the market price of the company's common stock. The phantom stock awards are typically taxed as ordinary income when vested, whether paid out or not. For accounting purposes, phantom stock is treated the same as deferred cash compensation. Similar to SARs, phantom stock can be appealing to closely held businesses.

Retirement Compensation

Extremely long-term compensation includes pension and OPEB. Pensions are commitments to provide retirement benefits to employees. Substantial accounting issues are associated with defined benefit plans that pay a periodic annuity over the life of the retiree. Multiple assumptions and calculation must be made and the rules associated with pensions change fairly often. The most recent requirements are based on SFAS No. 158, *Employers' Accounting for Defined Benefit Pension and Other Postretirement Plans.* Postretirement benefits are postemployment commitments such as health insurance. The rules also are complex and similar to pensions. Basic accounting associated with pensions and postemployment benefits are shown in Exhibit 3.3.

Exhibit 3.3 Pensions and Other Post-employment Benefits Entries

Defined Contribution Plans

More companies are switching and using defined contribution plans because they tend to be cheaper, the accounting is easy, and the company has no further obligations. Gotrocks contributes $50,000 to the 401(k) accounts of employees. Gotrocks matches employee contribution up to 6 percent of their annual salary, also $50,000. The entry was:

Pension expense	50,000
Cash	50,000

Gotrocks has no further obligation for employee retirement, except whatever contractual commitment exists to provide additional funding from year to year (such as Gotrocks commitment to match employee contributions up to 6 percent).

Defined Benefit Plans

Gotrocks started a defined benefit pension plan is 2014. The service cost for 2014 was $150,000, discount rate was 8 percent, and no pension assets existed. Because no pension coverage existed before 2014, there was no interest cost. (Gotrocks does not assume earlier pension commitments; that is, employees do not get *retirement credit* for employment before 2014.) Pension expense included only service costs for the year of $150,000 (determined by an actuarial consultant); the $150,000 also represent the pension benefits obligation (PBO) at year-end. The company invested an equivalent amount in the pension fund.

Pension expense	150,000
Cash	150,000

The pension fund invested the $150,000 cash in stocks and bonds and other investment securities on January 1, 2015. The expected return on plan assets was 10 percent; the calculation for 2015 was $150,000 \times 10\% = \$15,000$ (the expected return also reduces the pension expense for the year). The actual return was $16,000. The actual return increases plan assets but does not reduce pension expense, which is based on expected rather than actual return (the assumption being that actual return is too volatile from year to year to be meaningful). The interest cost for 2015 was $12,000 ($150,000 times 8 percent, the discount rate). The service cost was $160,000. Pension expense at year-end was calculated as:

Service cost	$160,000
Interest cost	$12,000
Expected return on plan assets	−$15,000
Pension expense	$157,000

Cash was paid to the pension plan in the same amount as pension expense for the year. The year-end journal entry was:

Pension expense	157,000
Cash	157,000

The calculations for PBO for year-end 2015 were:

PBO, beginning of the year	$150,000
+ Service cost for 2015	$160,000
+ Interest cost for 2015	$12,000
PBO, ending balance	$322,000

The fair value of plan assets for year-end 2015 was:

Fair value, beginning of the year	$150,000
+ Actual return on plan assets for 2015	$16,000
+ 2015 contributions to plan assets	$157,000
Fair value of plan assets, December 31, 2015	$323,000

The calculation of funded status, the net obligation the company has on the pension plan, was $1,000 (plan assets of $323,000 less PBO of $322,000), meaning that the plan is *overfunded* by $1,000.

Other Postretirement Benefit Plans (Health Care)

Gotrocks started a health coverage plan for future retiring employees at the start of 2014. The calculations and journal entries are similar to defined benefit pension plans. Because of IRS rules, the plan will not be funded by pension assets. Gotrocks recognized accumulated postretirement benefit obligations for health care from prior years of $50,000 on January 1 (which was determined on an actuarial basis by an outside consultant). The journal entry was:

Other comprehensive income-prior service cost	50,000
Accrued postretirement benefit cost	50,000

The $50,000 in obligations from past years when the plan was initiated in 2014 is treated as other comprehensive income (OCI); that is, they are expense- or loss-related costs that are attributed to past years rather than the current year.[9]

Over the year, the service cost was $1,800 (actuarially determined); interest cost was $5,000, calculated as beginning accrued postretirement benefit cost times the discount rate of 10 percent. These two costs ($1,800 + $5,000 = $6,800) represented OPEB costs for the year, as follows:

Postretirement benefit expense	6,800
Accrued postretirement benefit cost	6,800

The prior service costs, recorded as OCI, were accrued over five years ($50,000/5 = $10,000 a year) as a year-end accrual. The 2014 year-end entry was:

Accrued postretirement benefit cost	10,000
Other comprehensive income-prior service cost	10,000

The accumulated postretirement benefit obligation at year-end 2014 (recorded as a liability on the balance sheet) was calculated as follows:

Beginning balance	$50,000
+ Service cost	$1,800
+ Interest cost	$5,000
Balance, December 31, 2014	$56,800

Pensions

A pension is a contract to pay a fixed sum to a person, generally a monthly annuity after retirement. Pensions were initially (for accounting purposes) almost always *pay-as-you-go* defined benefit plans: A pension expense was recognized only for the actual pension cash payments (annuities) to employees. The concept of accruing pension expense associated with the actual work done by the employees to earn the pension began when the

Accounting Principles Board (APB—the predecessor body to the FASB) issued Opinion No. 8 in 1966, *Accounting for the Cost of Pension Plans*. The rules changed periodically, with the standard setters attempting to determine how to approximate economic reality dealing with this complex subject.

Defined benefit plans available to all employees are usually qualified pension plans, subject to Internal Revenue Service (IRS) regulations. The employers *qualify* for a tax deduction: Employer contributions to the plan are a tax deduction, pension earnings are exempt from taxes, and employer contributions are not taxable to the employees until they actually receive pension benefits. The retired employee normally pays tax on pension benefits received as ordinary income.

Under a defined benefit plan, the company has a long-term obligation to contractual payments over the lives of the retired employees, usually based on some combination of length of service and final pay. If an employee is guaranteed 2 percent of final pay for every year of service, she worked 30 years, and final pay was $100,000, the pension obligation is $60,000 a year ($100,000 × 30 × 2%). When and how many employees will retire, what their final pay is, and how long they will live are among the many items to be estimated. The company also will usually accumulate pension assets invested in stock, bonds, and other earning assets to fund these future obligations. Then it has to be determined how these estimates and calculations affect the current year's income statement and balance sheet. The employer manages the retirement fund, possibly though a specialty firm, to pay cash to retirees as the annuity payments come due, invests in pension assets, and determines all calculations to account for the complex activities. The company bears all the risk of the pension and must comply with all regulations, plus GAAP accounting and reporting requirements.

The plan assets are the portfolios of investment securities, stated at fair value (e.g., the closing market value of stock and other financial assets traded on public exchanges).The projected benefit obligation (PBO) is the present value of the total obligations to pay retirees based on services performed and expected future obligations (commitments based on expected future services, final salaries, and expected mortality, based on some discount rate).[10] Funded status is fair value of plan assets less PBO.

It is a reasonable estimate of the economic value at a particular point whether a pension is fully funded. If funded status is a net asset (plan assets are greater than PBO), the plan is overfunded; if funded status is a net liability, the plan is underfunded.

During the 1990s, most defined benefit pension plans were over-funded and plan assets were much larger than obligations. The market was pumped up by a stock bubble and under then-existing accounting rules, pension obligations were often understated. In the twenty-first century, most plans became underfunded. Partly it was the tech crash and the large drop in the stock market. Giroux (2006) reported that the 30 Dow Jones Industrial Average (DOW) firms showed pension overfunded in 2003 based on existing GAAP averaging at $4.6 billion; however, based on funded status, plans were underfunded at an average of $1.8 billion.[11] The FASB changed the reporting rules with SFAS No. 158, *Employers' Accounting for Defined Benefit Pension and Other Postretirement Plans—an Amendment of FASB Statements No. 87, 88, 106 and 132(R)*.

Corporations are subject to the Employment Retirement Income Security Act (ERISA) of 1974, the Pension Protection Act of 2006, and various IRS rules. Prior to ERISA, employees with defined benefit pension plans of companies that went bankrupt often lost most of their pension coverage (mainly because the plans were poorly funded). ERISA was established to protect the interests of employees. The Act established the Pension Benefit Guaranty Corporation (PBGC) to provide employee coverage from terminated pension plans (usually because of corporate bankruptcy). Essentially, the plan assets and obligations were transferred to the PBGC and some minimum level of pension payments was made to retirees. The Pension Protection Act of 2006 required pension plans to be fully funded (with complex requirements for underfunded plans).

Supplemental executive retirement plans (SERPs) are often available for executives in addition to retirement plans available to all employees. These are nonqualified plans, that is, not subject to IRS regulations (and not receiving tax benefits available to qualified plans), because they are specifically for executives rather than all employees. The covered exec-utives make no contributions to these plans. The funding is provided entirely by the company, but without IRS regulations, many alternatives exist. One option is cash value life insurance. In that case, the employer owns the policies, makes the coverage payments, and records any cash surrender value. If the employee dies, the company gets the cash proceeds and typically pays the employee's estate based on the contractual obligations.

Although the purpose of SERPs is to provide long-term incentives to valued executives, incentive-related problems exist. A SERP is a long-term commitment, often not related to actual performance. Until new SEC disclosure rules were issued in 2006, the costs of SERPs were basically hidden, a likely reason for their common use. Bebchuk and Jackson reviewed the importance of hidden compensation using the example of Franklin Raines, chief executive officer (CEO) of Fannie Mae, until being terminated at the end of 2004. After being pushed out, his executive pension was worth $1.4 million a year (a total value of about $24 million), a major part of his compensation and not tied to firm performance. Raines was fired after severe manipulation was uncovered by the auditors, with executive compensation a likely factor in encouraging fraud and abuse.[12,13]

Other Postemployment Benefits

Corporations often provide nonpension postretirement benefits (or benefits to terminated employees not retiring), and the category is called OPEB. Historically, like pension, these were recognized on a pay-as-you-go basis. Pension accounting shifted much earlier to an accrual basis, but OPEB accruals were recognized with SFAS No. 106, *Employers' Accounting for Postretirement Benefits Other Than Pensions*, issued in 1990. Consequently, companies went from ignoring all long-term OPEB liabilities on the balance sheet to full recognition, using accounting similar to that of pensions. Additional requirements were added by SFAS 132 (2003), *Employers' Disclosures about Pensions and Other Postretirement Benefits* and SFAS No. 158 (2006).

The most common benefits have been health and other forms of insurance. Because health care costs have escalated, these obligations have dramatically increased and have been a growing accounting concern. The underlying accounting has similar issues to defined benefit pension plans including estimation of future costs, payment requirements, and how these should be recognized on the current year's balance sheet and income statement. Because OPEB accounting and disclosures are similar to pensions, pension and OPEB disclosures are often presented in the same tables, as is the case with Pfizer (which is described in detail in Appendix 3).

Executive Compensation Disclosure

The SEC requires substantive disclosures of the senior executives, as described on the SEC website:

> The federal securities laws require clear, concise and understandable disclosure about compensation paid to CEOs, CFOs and certain other high-ranking executive officers of public companies. Several types of documents that a company files with the Commission include information about the company's executive compensation policies and practices. You can locate information about executive pay in: (1) the company's annual proxy statement; (2) the company's annual report on Form 10-K; and (3) registration statements filed by the company to register securities for sale to the public.

> In the annual proxy statement, a company must disclose information concerning the amount and type of compensation paid to its chief executive officer, chief financial officer and the three other most highly compensated executive officers. A company also must disclose the criteria used in reaching executive compensation decisions and the degree of the relationship between the company's executive compensation practices and corporate performance.

> The Summary Compensation Table is the cornerstone of the SEC's required disclosure on executive compensation. The Summary Compensation Table provides, in a single location, a comprehensive overview of a company's executive pay practices. It sets out the total compensation paid to the company's chief executive officer, chief financial officer and three other most highly compensated executive officers for the past three fiscal years. The Summary Compensation Table is then followed by other tables

and disclosure containing more specific information on the components of compensation for the last completed fiscal year. This disclosure includes, among other things, information about grants of stock options and stock appreciation rights; long-term incentive plan awards; pension plans; and employment contracts and related arrangements.[14]

Executive compensation disclosures are presented in the proxy statement (DEF 14A), the report issued before the annual shareholders' meeting. The purpose of the proxy statement is to present to the stockholders the information to vote on, including the directors (at most companies, the board members are voted for annually), the auditor and audit fees, and thanks to the Dodd-Frank bill, additional compensation information of senior executives and the board. Because most stockholders do not attend the meeting, they vote by proxy.

Selected executive compensation tables from the 2013 proxy statement of Microsoft (for fiscal year 2013) are presented in the Appendix 1 (with Microsoft's compensation disclosure from the 2013 10-K in Appendix 2). Microsoft is used as a reasonably typical large public corporation subject to the disclosure rules of the SEC.

Impact on Financial Statements

The major impact of the compensation entries is an increase in expenses (mainly operating expenses) offset by a reduction in cash and (mostly temporary) increases in current liabilities. Entries related to pension and other retirement benefits are more complicated and involve both short-term and long-term obligations and appropriate expensing. Defined contributions are expensed, offset to cash and short-term liabilities. Defined benefit plans include expenses for the current year costs, and long-term liabilities for future annuity obligations. In addition are cash contributions to invest in stock and bonds to create long-term investments from which to pay these future obligations (*plan assets*). Adjustments are made annually to the various long-term accounts to recognize current and future obligations. Similar entries are made to OPEB accounts associated with other current and future obligations such as health care for former employees. Given the long-term (and essentially permanent) nature of these obligations, long-term liabilities can be substantial. The underlying accounts involve complex calculations (mostly ignored in the example), plus changing rules. It is likely that pension and OPEB accounting rules have changed more over the years than any other accounting topic.

Stock options and stock-related grants such as restricted stock have complicated effects. One reason for option complexity is the changing rules, both accounting and tax. GAAP requirements changed with ASB 25, FASB 123, and FASB 123R. Journal entries for this chapter referred only to the current rules of FASB 123R, which require expensing of options when they are issued (plus additional entries when options are exercised—mainly increasing equity and cash).

Additional entries are required for benefits given exclusively to executives, included separate pensions, deferred compensation, and other contractual obligations with various executives. The individual entries generally are not complex, although the impact of taxes and other legal requirements can be important. The benefits to senior executives are particularly important because of the additional disclosure and voting requirements within the proxy statements.

CHAPTER 4

Historical Perspective on Executive Pay

In his 1936 State of the Union address, President Franklin D. Roosevelt railed against "entrenched greed" at American corporations. At the time, the average compensation for the top executives of a big company was about $95,000.

—Wall Street Journal

America evolved from an agrarian economy to an industrial powerhouse through the complex interactions of innovators, entrepreneurs, rule of law, a capitalist system, growing capital markets, and a rising class of professional managers. The chief executive officers (CEOs) mainly held ownership interests as founders, partners, and major stockholders. With industrial consolidation in the late nineteenth and early twentieth centuries, professional managers without major ownership interests became increasingly important, resulting in rising pay and experimentation in cash bonuses and equity interests. Executive pay rose sharply during the Roaring Twenties and then crashed with the economy in the Great Depression of the 1930s. With a sluggish economy and substantial regulations on business, executive pay remained flat or down. The early post–World War II period saw increased experimentation of executive compensation plans (stock options and other equity incentives, pensions, and various perquisites), but total compensation increased very slowly. A host of economic and regulatory changes resulted in more rapid executive pay rises from the mid-1970s. Finally, a perfect storm of regulatory and economic factors brought in exploding executive pay beginning in the 1990s, but this slowed down during the tech crash of the early twenty-first century and the subprime meltdown of 2008. The recovery since then suggests that CEO pay is back in expansion mode. Executive pay tends to be somewhat pro-cyclical, going up and down in the same direction as the business cycle.

Two recurring historical themes, in large part, determined the types and levels of pay: innovations in pay and regulations, not necessarily in that order. When industry introduced new types of compensation, the government and other regulators determined the rules on procedures and disclosures, how to tax compensation components, and how to account for them. Companies responded to the regulations by expanding their use, abandoning them, or changing them for more favorable treatment. The results were often unintended consequences, usually not what the regulators expected or desired. The changing use and rules on stock options represent the best evidence.

Owners, Entrepreneurs, and Management Professionals

Business owners and entrepreneurs have been around since the dawn of civilization. The ideas of professional managers mainly developed in the nineteenth century for railroads. Railroads have always been big businesses requiring outside capital and therefore absentee ownership. By the mid-nineteenth century, railroads were consolidating and becoming more professional. They had no choice. To stay in business they needed extensive management oversight. The early professional leaders were mainly engineers willing to spend a lifetime drawing a salary, possibly moving to a new railroad for a better, higher-paying job. Industrial firms such as oil, iron and steel, or food processing were mainly started and run by entrepreneurs with little help from Wall Street. Senior managers often were part owners, perhaps fellow entrepreneurs bought out by bigger competitors. Eventually, professional managers would fill more positions (including CEOs), and these firms would be listed by the New York Stock Exchange (NYSE) or other exchanges and securities would trade on Wall Street.

The movement to big business and the need for professional, salaried managers started after the Civil War. The country (especially the North) was booming and industrial demand continued to grow, fueled in part by bubbles and euphoria (but slowed down by periodic downturns). Industries consolidated to alleviate so-called cut-throat competition, especially during the recurring depressions. John D. Rockefeller's Standard Oil was a leader. Rockefeller faced competition willing to sell cheap, but often inferior products. Standard Oil turned ruthless in acquiring competitors or driving them out of business if they would not sell. Eventually, Standard Oil controlled some 90 percent of refining capacity and developed the legal means to operate across the country through the trust and later incorporation in New Jersey and other *charter mongering* states allowing corporations to own shares of other corporations.

Over 150 industries achieved monopoly or oligopoly power through consolidation. This allowed monopoly prices and various price and product conspiracies. On the other hand, big business operating plants across multiple states required competent managers and the use of sophisticated accounting and engineering practices. These same managers also contemplated appropriate compensation. The leaders in *maximizing compensation* developed various types of bonus plans and, by the 1920s, some two-thirds of America's largest public companies had some form of cash or stock bonus plans for executives. A substantial number of companies also used employee stock-purchase plans. The total compensation of corporate executives with bonuses was substantially higher than that in companies paying only a cash salary.

Compensation over the Last 75 Years

Figure 4.1 provides a quick summary of relative CEO salaries from 1936 through 2005 using inflation-adjusted (year 2000) dollars. The data come from Frydman and Saks, a 2010 academic study in *The Review of Financial Studies*, using multiple sources and not completely consistent over time (large-scale databases did not show up until the 1980s). Most of the data come from Securities and Exchange Commission (SEC) filings, where disclosures changed over time, plus various adjustments for the value of stock options, and so forth for about the 50 largest companies. Frydman and Saks[1] is particularly useful because it provided limited testing of long-term relationships that have usually been tested over much shorter windows. Many of the hypotheses consistent with later periods did not hold up when evaluated over the earlier period (generally 1936 to 1970); for example, executive compensation generally rose with increasing corporate market capitalization in the later periods, but not the earlier ones.

Median CEO compensation ($ millions)

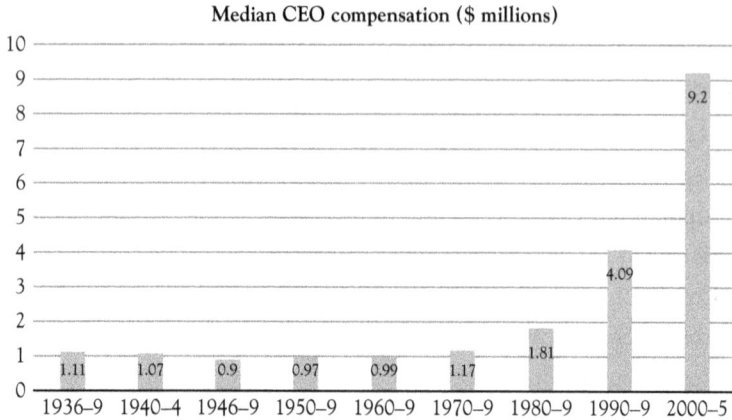

Figure 4.1 Average CEO Compensation, 1936–2005

Source: Adapted from Frydman and Saks (2010, 2113); numbers inflation adjusted to year 2000 prices.

Executive salaries remained flat to slightly down from the mid-1930s to the end of the 1960s. Compensation rose in the 1980s and exploded since the 1990s. Several economic theories (e.g., managerial power, efficient contracting) explain changes over a certain period but none can be generalized over this 70-year period. As summarized by Frydman and Saks:

> Prior to the 1970s, we observe low levels of pay, little dispersion across managers, weak correlation between pay and aggregate firm size, and a moderate degree of managerial incentives. Since then, salaries and incentive pay have grown dramatically, differences in pay across executive have widened, the correlation between compensation and aggregate firm size appears to have strengthened, and managerial incentives have gotten stronger.[2]

The best explanation seems to be given by Kevin Murphy attributing compensation changes (both amounts and types) to government policy—driven, in large part, by unintended consequences.[3]

The Early Years

The first experiments with bonuses and stock plans started early in the twentieth century. United States Steel and Bethlehem Steel began bonus plans in about 1902, shortly followed by stock awards given by Du Pont.

Alfred Sloan's (president and chairman of General Motors until 1956) memoir *My Years with General Motors* has an entire chapter called "Incentive Compensation," beginning with a cash bonus plan in 1918.

Historically, executive salaries were proprietary information; stockholders and other interested parties had no knowledge and therefore no outrage about amounts. That changed in the 1930s as a result of court cases, hearings, and regulatory action—then people got upset. In a lawsuit against Bethlehem Steel, it was disclosed that president W.R. Grace was paid over $1.6 million in salary in 1929 (the year of the Great Crash) and huge salaries were paid to executives during the 1920s despite the fact that Bethlehem did not pay dividends during those years. In a separate lawsuit, it was discovered that the American Tobacco president was scheduled to receive almost $2 million; as with Bethlehem, not disclosed to stockholders. The Congressional Pecora Commission[4] found that Charles Mitchell, the chairman and president of National City Bank, the nation's largest during the 1920s, received over $1 million a year in compensation from 1927 through 1929 and borrowed additional millions from the bank's *morale loan fund*, which did not require repayment. Mitchell was later indicted for tax evasion.

A particularly useful study of the early years was John Baker's *Executive Salaries and Bonus Plans* (1938), which looked at 100 major corporations listed on the NYSE from 1928 to 1936. This was based primarily on an analysis of compensation data gathered by the Federal Trade Commission (FTC) from 1928 to 1933 and disclosures required by the SEC from 1934 to 1936. The FTC analysis followed the public outrage at Bethlehem Steel, American Tobacco, and the Pecora Commission. As stated by Baker: "Probably the real reason that Congress forced the publication of salary data was the conscious or unconscious indictment of business leaders, both by the public and by many stockholders, for having failed in their fiduciary relationships with stockholders."[5]

The presidents' compensation of 100 large companies listed on the NYSE had a median total salary in 1929 of $69,728, seemingly a not unreasonable amount (about $940,000 in 2013 dollars). Sixty-eight had salaries of $100,000 or less. However, at the top of the list was Bethlehem's Grace, making $1,635.753 (over $22 million in 2013 dollars). Bethlehem's presidential salary declined to $180,000 by 1932. With the Great Depression, executive compensation fell. By 1932, the bottom of the depression, presidents' salaries averaged $41,833, a drop of 40 percent from 1929. As the economy improved from 1933 to 1936 (during Franklin D. Roosevelt's first term), average president's salary increased to $50,200 (up 20 percent from 1932).[6]

Particularly important for later comparisons was the use of bonuses and other forms of compensation. In addition to a base salary, executives could be paid cash bonuses, cash and stock bonuses (apparently no companies paid stock bonuses without also paying cash bonuses), and options or warrants. Bonuses were paid by 64 percent of the 100 companies analyzed by Baker in 1928, which dropped to 26 percent by 1932, the bottom of the depression. Of the 59 large companies with enough data for Baker to analyze in detail, 34 (57.6 percent) paid cash bonuses, 13 (22.0 percent) paid both cash and stock bonuses, and 12 (20.3 percent) paid no bonuses.[7] In addition, 35 (59.3 percent) had an employee stock purchase plan. In almost all cases, bonuses were based on some calculation of earnings. Companies using bonus plans paid out larger compensation packages than those that did not.

In 1929, companies with bonus plans paid out the equivalent 4.2 percent of earnings; those that did not paid 1.6 percent. The presidents of bonus-paying companies had an average total compensation in 1929 of $196,000, while those receiving cash only got an average of $80,000 (i.e., 41 percent as much). During the early 1930s, the salaries for bonus-paying companies dropped much faster than those of salary-only companies. By 1932, bonus-paying presidents had compensation averaging $80,000, compared to $64,000 at cash-only companies. As stated by Baker: "There is no evidence that the use of bonus plans lowered the regular cash salaries paid executives."[8] Virtually all bonus-paying companies also paid dividends to shareholders; only three paid executives bonuses and no dividends.[9]

The evidence from this early period provides initial evidence of recurring themes over the last century of executive compensation. First is the existence of extreme cases that outraged the public, but not necessarily representative of typical companies. Much of the legislation and regulation of business seems to be the result of this public outrage, typically fueled by the media. One possible reason for large compensation differences in this early period was the lack of knowledge of what the competition paid out, because it was proprietary information. The good news is that investigation and regulations led to disclosures that could be evaluated more scientifically. SEC-required disclosures of executive compensation have been available since 1934.

The Great Depression through the Post–World War II Period

The stock market collapsed in October 1929, after a major bubble driven by deception and manipulation. Early government action such as maintaining the gold standard (and high interest rates) and the Smoot–Hawley Tariff (raising tariff rates, causing retaliation) turned a downturn into the Great Depression. The Senate Banking and Currency Committee investigated through the Pecora Commission. The Commission uncovered massive manipulation and illicit financial practices, including million-dollar banker salaries and tax evasion. Public outrage led to the election of Franklin D. Roosevelt as president and the Democrats sweeping both houses of Congress. The first 100 days of the New Deal brought dozens of new organizations and programs attempting to fix the various problems in agriculture, unemployment, banking, Wall Street, and the corporate world. The most important dealing with executive compensation and accounting disclosures was the securities acts of 1933 and 1934.

Roosevelt's New Deal did not end the Great Depression—mistakes committed mainly in 1936 and later reversed the economic progress in the early Roosevelt years. It would take World War II to end the depression and create the environment for what became American prosperity and dominance. The strict government rules created during the 1930s were enforced and worked reasonably well through the first couple of decades of the post–World War II period. Executive compensation remained fairly tame (and actually declined compared to measures of average worker pay). Companies mainly followed the rules; the economy and stock market mostly went up. Despite many problems (racism, women's rights, the Cold War), this period was in some respects viewed as a golden age of economic activity.

The SEC

Regulating financial markets became part of the early New Deal agenda, following public and Congressional outrage about corporate fraud, market manipulation, and extreme executive compensation. Initial draft legislation concentrated on both new stock issues (initial public offerings or IPOs) and regulating the stock exchanges, both difficult issues. First up was the focus on new securities, with the first draft developed by a team under Felix Frankfurter, then a Harvard law professor and later a Supreme Court Justice. The primary focus on the legislation was full public disclosure of relevant information.

The Securities Act of 1933 (also called the Truth in Securities Act) was passed at the end of May, 1933. According to the SEC webpage, the purpose of the act was: "(1) require that investors receive financial and other significant information concerning securities being offered for public sale; and (2) prohibit deceit, misrepresentation, and other fraud in the sale of the securities."[10] A formal registration process was required including substantial disclosures as part of the prospectus. The authority for enforcing the Act was initially under the FTC. Now the business community was outraged by *overregulation*—or so they claimed.

Next up was the regulation of stock exchanges, almost immediately opposed by NYSE President Richard Whitney, later convicted and jailed for embezzlement. A major debate was whether to maintain jurisdiction with the FTC (as favored by the House of Representatives and President Roosevelt) or a new organization specializing in public securities (favored by the Senate). The Senate version won the day and the SEC Act of 1934, signed into law in June 1934, created the SEC, with broad powers over the securities industry, prohibitions over certain types of illicit activities, and financial reporting by public companies.

Almost from the beginning the SEC required annual reporting on executive compensation. In December 1934, the SEC demanded disclosure of the names and total compensation of the three highest-paid executives—those not complying would be delisted from stock exchanges. This comprehensive reporting of compensation began in 1935. Executive compensation has been disclosed in some forms in the corporations' 10-K[11] or annual proxy statement ever since (the specific requirements changed fairly regularly—major changes occurring in 1978, 1993, 2006, and 2011). The business media, beginning with *The New York Times*, *Forbes*, and *Business Week*, offered annual lists of the highest-paid executives—public exasperation usually followed.[12]

World War II and Beyond

It took World War II to get America out of the Great Depression. The war in Europe started with the German invasion of Poland in 1938. By 1940, most of Europe was under German control, with Great Britain being the major holdout. The Nazis attacked the Soviet Union in 1941. America's contribution was mainly *lend lease*, shipping goods to Britain and the USSR, while trying to remain neutral. The United States entered the war when Pearl Harbor was attacked on December 7, 1941. It was the industrial might of the United States that made victory possible, the vast industrial base producing military equipment. Mobilization required high taxes, spending, and borrowing.

As with all wars, war profiteering scandals were common. Senator Harry S. Truman headed the Special Committee to Investigate the National Defense Program, called the Truman Committee. Truman discovered faulty equipment and massive overcharges, one reason for the passage of an excess profit tax, rising to 90 percent. Another way to discourage war profiteering was to impose limits on executive pay increases and high taxes. The Stabilization Act of 1942 froze wages for all workers including executives, expiring in 1946. The top individual income tax rate rose to 94 percent in 1944. The major tax innovation was personal income tax withholding with the Pay-as-You-Go Act of 1943. Taxpayers found deductions from each paycheck more tolerable than the lump-sum payments previously required. Although there was a major shortage of executive talent in the private sector during World War II, few mechanisms existed to reward executive skills. Mainly, executives were given more tax-exempt perquisites such as improved health insurance and pension benefits.

At the end of World War II, with most developed countries in ruins, America dominated the economic world, producing half the globe's output. Although subject to recessions and other shocks, gross domestic product (GDP) exploded, from \$227.8 billion in 1946 to \$2.86 trillion in 1980—some 1,257 percent (up 204 percent on a real GDP per capital basis). The stock market also did well. The DOW rose from a 1946 low of 162 to over 1,000 in 1972 (and stayed roughly in the range of 600 to 1,000 during the 1970s decade). Despite the economic and stock market growth, executive compensation hardly changed (when adjusted for inflation). Average real salaries were actually lower during the 1960s than during 1936 to 1939 (see Figure 4.1). High income tax rates and regulations affecting the various pay components were partial explanations.

The Great Compression

This was the period of the *Great Compression* (roughly the 1940s to the 1970s) when average worker salaries rose as executive salaries fell or were stagnant.[13] Executive compensation stagnation seems unexpected because American corporations were profitable and world industrial leaders, with earnings and stock prices rising rapidly. Three reasons may be partial explanations. First, labor unions were relatively powerful and demanded substantial pay and benefit increases for blue-collar workers, while denouncing executive *excess*. In addition, there was an increased demand for unskilled and semi-skilled workers. During World War II, for example, over 113,000 General Motors employees left the company to join the military.[14] Second, the top tax rates were extremely high, above 90 percent from World War II until 1964 and at 70 percent until 1982. Third, there was no accommodating rules or regulations that made expansion of executive pay particularly desirable. World War II and Korean War regulations kept executive wages down, while more flexibility was allowed for ordinary workers (including minimum wages that were increased with increments from \$0.25 an hour in 1938 to \$0.75 in 1950). Later legislation was more favorable to executives, but not enough to have a great impact on pay.

Government's Role

The government's role promoting income compression was varied, and many of the consequences of legislation and regulation were unintended.

The most influential was taxes, both the rates on income tax and capital gains, but also what would qualify for the lower capital gain rates plus various seemingly obscure rules affecting such things as stock options, retirement benefits, or perquisites. New Deal legislation of the 1930s was favorable to labor, which encouraged worker income increases especially for labor union members. The SEC's required executive compensation disclosures probably discouraged pay hikes. World War II brought outrage over the potential for *war profiteering* by corporations. In addition, many corporate executives worked for government agencies to help mobilize the war effort as *dollar-a-year men* (i.e., unpaid)—making it difficult for other executives to demand pay increases.

The 16th Amendment allowed personal income tax by the federal government beginning in 1913. A major reason for support was the demand to tax the rich corporate Robber Barons of the period driving up income inequality. Congress and the Internal Revenue Service (IRS) broke new ground and had to determine what was taxable and at what rate. Ordinary income is just about any taxable income not considered long-term capital gains (or given some special favorable rate). Generally, capital gains are profits from the sale of noninventory assets such as securities or fixed assets.

The top tax rates (for both ordinary income and capital gains) rose to 77 percent during World War I. (The top rates are summarized by year in Figure 4.2.) The capital gains rate stayed at the ordinary income rate until 1922, and it has remained lower except for the short period 1988 to 1990 when both were at 28 percent. Rates dropped in the mid-1920s to 25 percent (12.5 percent for capital gains), and then rose in 1932 to 63 percent at the height of the Great Depression. Rates stayed high throughout the Great Compression (over 90 percent from 1944 through 1963), while capital gains remained fairly low at 25 percent (1943 to 1967). Executives had little incentive for pay increases unless they were untaxed (certain perquisites) or taxed at the capital gain rate (stock options at various times).

Labor got big breaks from New Deal legislation of the mid-1930s, especially the Wagner Act of 1935, which vastly increased the power of labor unions. When labor shortages hit with World War II and after, labor was in a position to demand real salary increases. The 1949 Treaty

Top tax rates

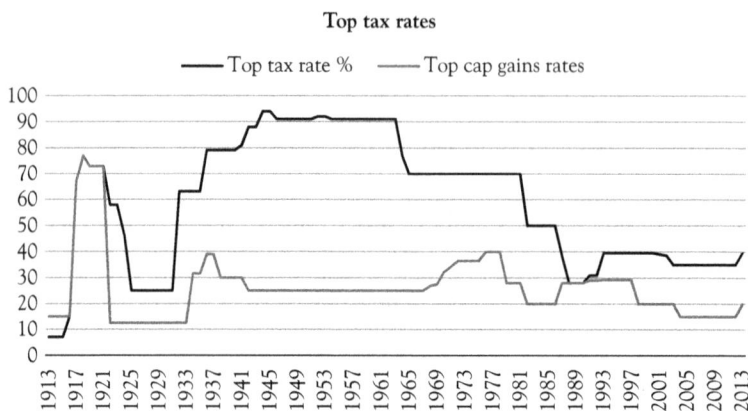

Figure 4.2 Top individual income tax and capital gains rates by year

Note: Rates include surcharges and other adjustments.
Source: Top individual income rates: Tax Foundation (www.taxfoundation.org), ordinary; capital gains rates: www.taxpolicycenter.org, capital gains (from 1954); citizens for tax justice (www.cfj.org/pdf/regcg.pdf), from 1913 to 1953.

of Detroit was a watershed moment in labor power.[15] Although the Taft-Hartley Act of 1947 restricted labor power, it was decades before the Act was effectively used against labor. Once inflation rose, foreign competition kicked in, unemployment increased during the 1970s, and labor power eroded.

An additional, if unusual, feature of government action was the wage freeze, common in the time of war, but also used by President Nixon in 1971. The Stabilization Act of 1942 froze wages during World War II (and expired in 1946), and the Salary Stabilization Board (1951 to 1952) limited executive pay increase during the Korean War. In August 1971, Nixon established a freeze on salaries and commodity prices, followed in December 1971 (phase two of the price or wage control) by a Pay Board that limited executive pay increase to 5.5 percent. The wage or price controls were the first during peace time. Various exemption and loopholes soon became evident, but median cash compensation increased at 4.5 percent in 1971, staying below Nixon's 5.5 percent (but were larger in 1972 and 1973). These not-very-successful controls expired in 1974.

Stock Options

A stock option (call) is a derivative contract giving the holder the right to buy a specific quantity of an asset at a specific price for a certain period.

A rationale for giving stock options to executives and employees is the incentives of ownership—a more successful company results in greater long-term compensation.[16] Early in the twentieth century, corporation occasionally gave stock options to executives, usually as part of compensation packages to entice them from other companies. The difficulty was observed in how they fit into tax law. Would they be taxed as capital gains or ordinary income? When would they be taxed? When vested? Exercised? Sold? Executives, initially without specific rules, would use the most favorable rates and timing, usually capital gain rate at the time they were sold. A 1946 Supreme Court case ruled that the profit should be taxed when exercised at the ordinary income rate, making options unappealing.

A business-friendly Republican Congress passed the Revenue Act of 1950, which created *restricted stock options*. To be considered *restricted*, the options had to have an exercise price at least 95 percent of the stock's price at the grant date, must be held by the recipient for at least two years before being exercised, and then held at least six months before being sold. If all these conditions were met, the profit would be taxed at the capital gain rate: 25 percent throughout 1950 versus over 90 percent for ordinary income over $200,000.[17] By the early 1960s, the majority of firms on the NYSE handed out options and stock options accounted for 48 percent of the total pay for the highest-paid executives in 1963.[18] As shown in Figure 4.1, the expanded use of stock options hardly made a dent in inflation-adjusted total executive pay.

The favorable tax treatment of options was called into question by the Kennedy administration in the early 1960s and Congressional hearings. The result was the Revenue Act of 1964, which created *qualified stock options* in place of *restricted options*, with requirements that were much less attractive.[19] The 1964 Act also lowered the top tax rate to 70 percent, making ordinary income relatively more attractive. The Tax Reform Act of 1969 basically eliminated the remaining attractive features of qualified stock options by lowering the top rate to 50 percent and increasing the capital gains rate to 35.5 percent.

Another factor in the limited impact of options was the secular bear market (10 to 20 years of relatively stagnant stock prices) from the mid-1960s to the early 1980s, in part because of rising stagflation (inflation, high unemployment, and stagnant economic growth).[20] Figure 4.3a shows stock market trends for 1930 to 1980 as measured by the DOW.

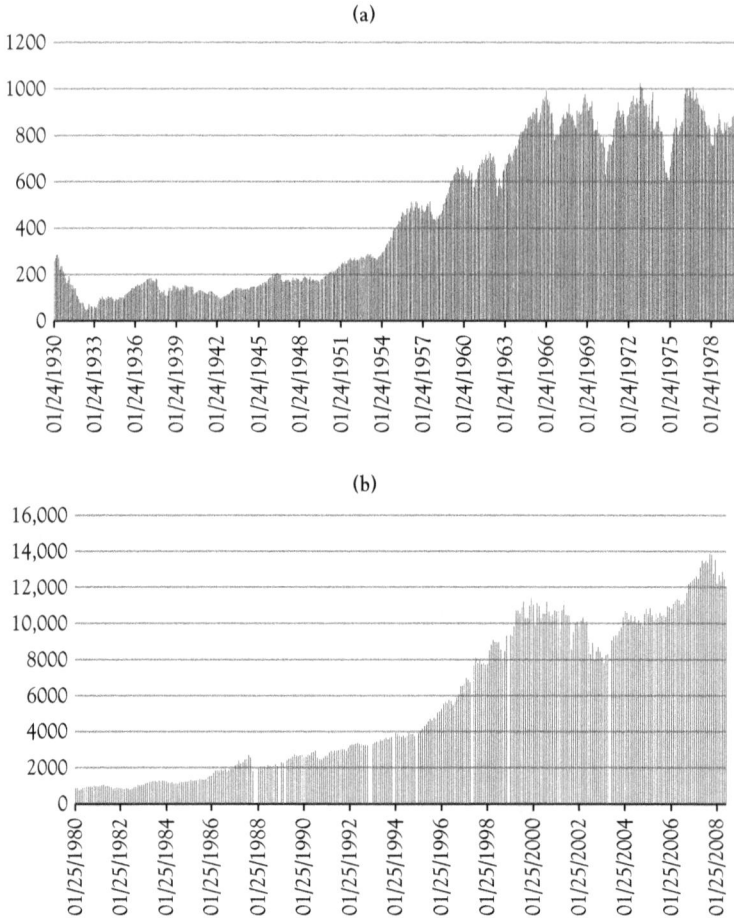

Figure 4.3 *Stock prices over half a century: (a) DOW (1930–1980) and (b) DOW (1980–2008)*

Two secular bear markets (1930 to the early 1950s and 1966 to 1980) as well as a secular bull market in between are obvious. Stock options would eventually become the largest component of executive compensation, but this trend would not start until the 1980s.

The Great Divergence

The Great Compression came to an end in the 1980s (with the 1970s began a transition period of stagflation) along with the convergence of the Reagan Revolution, low inflation, reduced income tax rates, the decline in labor power, American industry becoming more competitive in world markets, and a bull market in stocks. Economist Paul Krugman dubbed this the "Great Divergence."[21] The wealthy were on the road to super riches, median income stagnated, and executive compensation grew and then exploded upward. The explanations for these major changes are widespread, from economic conditions, to a large range of laws and regulations, and the evolving business culture.

Economic conditions included the decline of unions and labor power as well as the rise of global competition. Wall Street and investment banks became stronger, more aggressive, and used *financial innovations* to increase market share and profits. Laws and regulations included changing tax rates, plus changing philosophies of taxation and the role of government in business. Deregulation started in the 1970s and became a major theme of the Reagan presidency. Somewhat surprising, deregulations continued (especially in financial markets) pretty much nonstop, except for the political reactions to Enron/tech collapse and the subprime meltdown of 2008. A culture of greed became more prominent and increasingly successful, while CEOs became less susceptible to the *outrage constraint*.

Transition—1970s

In 1970, Richard Nixon was the president, the Vietnam War was still the major headline, the stock market was bearish, plus the economy was in the doldrums and starting on the path to stagflation (both double-digit inflation and unemployment simultaneously before the decade was over). Government or regulatory action impacted executive compensation incentives during the decade. Nixon withdrew from the gold-exchange standard in 1971 and attempted wage and price controls. The energy crisis hit with the oil embargo of 1973. The misery index (inflation rate plus unemployment rate) remained in double digits from 1973 through 1985. The top personal income tax rate was 70 percent throughout the decade (but down from 91 percent), while the capital gain rate varied but remained over 30 percent (in other words, about half the ordinary income rate).

The SEC required public companies to disclose total compensation of top executives beginning in 1935 (although *Forbes* did not start its annual survey of the highest-paid CEOs until 1970). Two possible hypotheses can be stated about these disclosures. First is the *shame factor*; the act of disclosure would embarrass executives from receiving high salaries and substantial raises. Employees, especially union members, could be outraged if the CEO received fabulous compensation, while they were expected to receive less. On the other hand, executives could now compare their pay package to those of competitors. Particularly those who have no shame might want to lead the list or at least not suffer from being below their salary expectations. Beginning in this transition period of the 1970s and early 1980s, apparently fewer and fewer executives suffered much from the shame factor.

The Nixon resignation in 1974 after the Watergate scandal did not bode well for the popularity of politicians, especially his replacement Gerald Ford. After the presidential pardon of Nixon and poor economic conditions, Ford was defeated by Jimmy Carter in 1976. Carter's own severe energy and economic problems (not to mention his *malaise speech*) —with the misery index around 20 percent—led to his defeat and the election of the ebullient Republican Ronald Reagan in 1980. The Great Divergence would be well underway during the Reagan Revolution.

Reagan Revolution—1980s

Taking office in 1981, Reagan faced stagflation, energy shortages, and other economic problems (plus the *Evil Empire*). The tough love of Federal Reserve Chairman Paul Volcker kept interest rates high and the economy weak. In the meantime, Reagan called for much lower taxes and deregulation. The Volcker strategy worked, with inflation rates dropping from 13.5 percent in 1980 to 3.2 percent by 1983, an economic recovery, and the misery index falling below 10 percent by 1986. Volcker was replaced as Fed Chair by Doctor Deregulation, Alan Greenspan, in 1987. Soon after taking office, Greenspan faced the stock crash of 1987, when the DOW dropped 23 percent on October 19, 1987. He bailed out the market with billions in cash. He would repeat these bailouts several times, despite his belief in deregulation.

At the top of the Reagan agenda were tax cuts. First up was a reduction in rates. The Economic Recovery Act of 1981 reduced the top individual tax rate to 50 percent and the capital gain rate to 20 percent. Unfortunately, there were not enough expenditure cuts to reduce the growing budget deficit. During Reagan's second term, the Tax Reform Act of 1986 was a major overhaul, eliminating most deductions but reducing the top rate to 28 percent. Because of growing deficits, the top rate was increased to 31 percent in 1991 and 39.6 percent in 1993. The key point was much lower tax rates for executives making big bucks and, since they kept more of their total compensation, incentives to make even more money.

Part of the story was the continuing decline of the power of labor. When air traffic controllers went on strike in 1981, Reagan fired a lot of them—11,000. Flights were more or less maintained by supervisors and nonstriking controllers, and the union was decertified. The power of unions continued to decline, in large part because of foreign competition, the ability of many employers to move operations south or out of the country, the related strategy of foreign outsourcing, plus the potential failure of the big rust-belt industries such as autos and steel. Powerful unions were often able to slap down overly generous executive pay packages, while demanding good wage and benefit increases. As unions lost power, they became increasingly frustrated and impotent.

With low inflation and reduced tax rates, the economy and stock markets boomed. The DOW at the end of the 1980s decade tripled from the beginning (from 876 at the start of the chart to 2,709—see Figure 4.3). Unlike earlier decades, top executives started to participate in this bull market—which exploded up past 10,000 by the start of the new millennium. From 1980 to 1992, median total real CEO compensation for 500 large corporations doubled from $946,000 to $1,900,000, with almost half the compensation from stock options.[22] Of course, a bull market means that the value of options continues to rise and the share of compensation received from options can increase substantially.

The Great Explosion—1990s

In 1990, George H.W. Bush was the president, but a tax increase (after his "read my lips, no new taxes" pledge) and a short recession doomed his reelection. Bill Clinton became president in 1993. Clinton became a deregulation, balanced-budget champ and rode the tech wave to euphoria and a bubble. CEOs and other executives rode the same wave to gargantuan salaries. A perfect storm of factors hit about the same time to propel executive compensation into the stratosphere. The Reagan Revolution provided low taxes and an emphasis on free market politics. An influential article by economists Michael Jensen and Kevin Murphy preached the need for performance-based CEO pay. The Clinton administration and Congress passed the 1993 Revenue Reconciliation Act, which capped corporate salaries at $1 million as tax deductible, but allowed unlimited performance-based salaries. Activist shareholders (such as pension funds) also began to demand performance-based CEO pay. New accounting and disclosure rules at the time favored stock options and other stock-based compensation.

Jensen and Murphy's 1990 *Harvard Business Review* article, "CEO Incentives—It's Not How Much You Pay, But How," claimed that CEOs were generally paid "like bureaucrats." That is, compensation was not based specifically on performance. A $1,000 increase in share value in the 1980s was associated with only a $2.59 increase in CEO pay. Although about half the pay was bonuses; both bonuses and total compensation did not significantly vary with the share value. Their empirical analysis demonstrated that average CEO compensation at public companies adjusted for inflation in the mid-1980s was, in fact, less than that in the mid-1930s ($843,000 versus $882,000—in 1988 dollars). Jensen and Murphy claimed that CEOs' share ownership was too low for efficient contracting based on "pay-performance sensitivity." In their view, stock options had the necessary "value-increasing incentives."

Corporate American bought into this Jensen and Murphy framework, as did shareholder activists, Wall Street, and some Washington politicians. (Much of the public thought executives were vastly overpaid.) The initial idea of the Revenue Reconciliation Act of 1993 was that compensation above $1 million was unreasonable, but the Clinton administration backtracked, agreeing that exceptions for executives increasing productivity could be rewarded. The Act seemed to be antibusiness, raising the top individual tax rate to 39.6 percent and limiting corporate pay deduction of executives to $1 million. The intent was to restrain CEO pay, but the final rules proved to be a boon to executives because compensation linked to company performance was unlimited. The IRS wrote the rules on what performance-based meant and these proved to be accommodating to executives, including stock options (with an exercise price equal to or greater than market price at grant date), formula-driven bonus payments, and other performance-based restricted stock and related equity payments.[23]

The floodgates were open to exploding compensation at the top as CEOs, directors, and consultants invented new ornaments for the compensation tree—after more and more corporations increased base CEO salary to the $1 million cap. New compensation items were added on to existing contracts (often based on the rationale of better incentive matching) rather than replacing other items. Median CEO pay adjusted for inflation more than tripled from 1992 to 2001 for the S&P 500, from $2.9 million to $9.3 million. The major driver was the escalation of stock options.[24] It was the combination of shovel loads of options and the growing Tech Bubble that pushed options to the major compensation component.

Options proved to be one of many accounting issues that defied resolution and new pronouncements were issued regularly. In the case of options, the major reasons were the complexity of the calculations and intense lobbying by corporations for favorable rules. New rules were being developed by the Financial Accounting Standards Board (FASB) in the early 1990s, with the intent of requiring corporations to record the value of options as a compensation expense based on the Black-Scholes or other models of option pricing. Former SEC Chairman Arthur Levitt stated: "Whenever the FASB tried to crack down by tightening accounting standards, it ran into a phalanx of corporate, Congressional, and auditor opposition."[25] Levitt advised the FASB to water down the new pronouncement, which it did.[26] Statement of Financial Accounting Standards (SFAS) No. 123, issued in 1995, allowed companies to (1) expense the options based on an options pricing model or (2) record no expense, but present pro forma disclosures in a footnote showing the impact on net income as if an options pricing model had been used. Most companies used the second alternative, viewing options as *costless*. The IRS, on the other hand, allowed a tax deduction to the corporation for options when exercised.

Options took on the mantle of the most important compensation source and corporations issued massive amounts.[27] From 1991 to 2001, the percent of options granted by the S&P 500 to employees rose from 1.1 percent of total shares outstanding to 2.6 percent, while the average grant value of options rose from $27 million to $287 million over the

CEO Pay

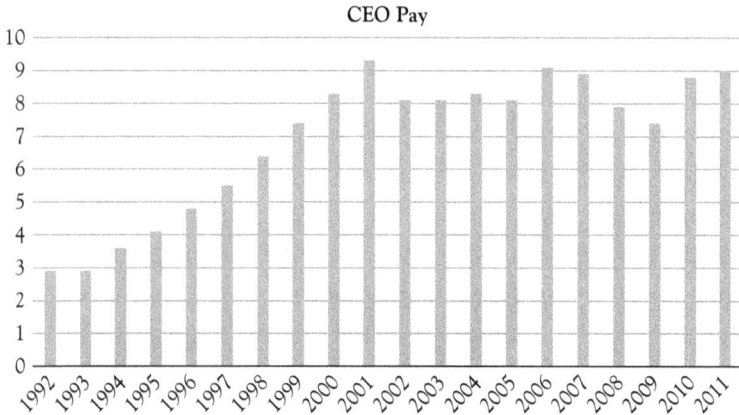

Figure 4.4 *Median chief executive officer (CEO) compensation,*
1992–2011, S&P 500 firms (2011 dollars)
Source: Adapted from Murphy (2012, 73 and 97).

same period (based on 2011 dollars)—worth a total $800 billion across
the 500 firms.[28] The result was CEO pay for the S&P 500 that more
than tripled in less than a decade to an average of over $9 million (see
Figure 4.4).

Collapse of the Tech Bubble

Despite all the claims that it was indeed different this time, the market
collapsed after the turn of the new millennium. Perhaps, the most amazing thing was the degree of scandals and corruption involved, even with
all the regulation and failsafe mechanisms: board regulations—executives
paid substantial compensation presumably aligned with shareholders,
complex accounting and disclosure rules, stringent financial audits, substantial SEC reviews, stock exchange requirements, and a sophisticated
financial press.

The Tech Bubble was a speculative stock run up mainly involving
computer- and Internet-based firms, many of which were listed on
National Association of Security Dealers Automated Quotations (NAS-
DAQ). The NASDAQ 100 hit 1,000 in 1995 (up from 100 in 1971),
rising to a high of 5,049 in March 2000. The collapse came soon after and
the index dropped to 1,114 in October 2002, down about 80 percent.
Big and small companies proceeded to fail, suffering from over-leverage,

manipulation, and fraud. Among the failures were Global Crossing, Tyco, Quest, Imclone, Adelphia, and WorldCom.

At the top of the list was the bankruptcy of Enron at the end of 2001, the largest failure in American history up to that time. After numerous investigations and Congressional hearing, it was demonstrated that Enron was a seriously corrupt company, using a variety of sophisticated fraud tools to game the earnings numbers. The executive compensation incentives proved too irresistible to play by the rules. As I summarized in an earlier article:

> The Enron story is a useful microcosm of all that could go wrong with high-tech business and the motivation for the stock market bubble of the late 1990s. This includes executive greed, ruthlessness, a lack of ethical standards, accommodating auditors, law firms and investment bankers, lack of proper regulatory oversight, substantial political contributions used to acquire influence in Washington, and a derelict board of directors. The stodgy gas transmission company remade itself as a high tech conglomerate and, despite obvious high leverage and extreme financial risks, misled investors on its true value for years.[29]

Enron was the seventh largest company in America by market value in 2000, propelled by a massive set of complex frauds. Fair value measurements were abused, gas traders manipulated markets, traders moved to other markets such as electricity to manipulate further, and special purpose entities (SPEs) were established to claim virtually any amount of revenue, cost reduction, or removal of debt to meet the current quarter's needed numbers. In 2000, Chairman and CEO Kenneth Lay had a base salary and bonus of over $8 million plus 782,000 stock options. He also exercised $123 million in options. Lay's contract (which was similar to that of other senior executives) called for a 15 percent annual growth of earnings. His hundreds of thousands of options (other executives had smaller amounts but similar incentives) did not vest unless the earnings targets were continuously met. Thanks to relentless fraud and cozy compensation contracts, Enron paid over half a billion dollars to executives from 1996 to 2000.

Meeting financial analysts' quarterly earnings forecasts was a must. This was accomplished by an ever-increasing use of sophisticated fraud, especially the deceptive use of SPEs run by the Chief Financial Officer (CFO) Andrew Fastow. Fastow was a crook in his own right, siphoning off millions from Enron by becoming the *equity investor* in a multitude of fraudulent SPEs. After auditor Arthur Andersen forced Enron to restate earnings by over a billions dollars in 2001, bankruptcy could not be avoided—to the complete shock of the investment world. Even around the bankruptcy event, illicit activities continued. Although 4,500 Enron employees were fired, Enron gave $55 million in bonuses to *key* executives. Lay and co-conspirators bailed out of their vested stock options during 2001, while encouraging employees to continue to hold on to their options and shares. Few tears were shed when some 30 Enron executives were charged and most convicted of criminal acts, beginning with Ken Lay.

Enron was not alone. Multiple corporate accounting scandals were discovered about the same time. The SEC and Justice Department investigated while Congress held hearings, beginning within days of the Enron bankruptcy. Enron executives were called to testify and most pled the fifth as cameras rolled. The House Financial Services Committee and the Senate Government Affairs Committee worked on reform legislation, but reform zeal petered out until WorldCom went under in mid-2002, replacing Enron for the biggest bankruptcy in American history. Reform legislation was back on the table.

The Sarbanes-Oxley Act (SOX) was passed within days of the World-Com bankruptcy and signed into law on July 30, 2002. SOX was the most substantial reform since the Securities Acts of the 1930. New corporate governance requirements were put in place to encourage better board oversight, a new independent audit regulator was created (the Public Company Accounting Oversight Board or PCAOB), and various requirements of executives, the SEC, stock exchanges, and other regulators put into place. Although SOX was aimed at preventing future accounting scandals, modest executive compensation-related rules were included. Section 402 prohibited personal loans to executives and directors (before SOX, often used to buy company stock). Section 304 required CEO and CFO clawbacks for performance-based compensation (bonuses and equity based) if the financial statements were restated for "corporate misconduct."

Moderation—2000s

Recession followed corporate scandals and market plunges, which was quite effective at reducing executive compensation, at least temporarily. Most compensation falls dramatically for the cheaters getting caught (to zero for some in bankruptcy). Corporate boards are less likely to approve outrageous bonuses and stock awards when earnings tank, and stock value drops reduce the value of outstanding options and other equity compensation. As expected, executive compensation dropped for a while after 2000. Given the backlash against options from the tech bust scandals, the average value of stock options to S&P 500 employees (in 2011 dollars) fell from $287 million in 2000 to $88 million in 2005 (down $199 million or 69.3 percent). Total median CEO compensation (also in 2011 dollars) dropped more modestly, from $9.3 million in 2001 to $8.1 million in 2005 (down 12.9 percent)[30] (see Figure 4.4).

Despite SOX, corporate misconduct continued. Among the post-SOX scandals were stock option backdating, spring loading, and speed vesting. Research by Erik Lie in 2005 discovered that options were often granted on dates when the stock price bottomed, an unexpected practice unless companies were backdating options to this low point to raise recipients' gains. Reporting by the *Wall Street Journal* led to SEC investigation of 140 firms. The SEC filed civil charges against 66 people in 24 companies for option backdating. In another move of questionable ethics (but generally legal) called spring loading, many companies issued options in anticipation of future good news (such as the announcement of a new product) or issue options after a major price drop. Many companies, for example, issued options shortly after 9/11 when stock prices dropped substantially.

The FASB revised FAS 123 in 2004 (as SFAS 123R, *Accounting for Stock-based Compensation*). This time, all public firms were required to treat stock options as a compensation expense based on Black-Scholes or another pricing model beginning with the 2006 fiscal year. This made options much less appealing and many companies switched to restricted stock or other equity-based compensation. Two major events occurred. First, many companies changed vesting requirements to 2005, in other words, before 123R went into effect—speed vesting. Second, restricted stock soon replaced stock options as the largest source of executive compensation.[31]

In the meantime, banks and shadow banks were busy creating the next bubble, based on mortgages and structured finance. With investment grade ratings and higher interest rates than Treasury bonds, mortgage-backed securities (MBSs) had almost unlimited demand. Given the performance-based pay in the finance industries, predatory practices were used to increase the mortgage supply, including subprime, liar loans and exploding adjustable rate mortgages. Fueled by seemingly unlimited credit, housing prices across the country roughly doubled. The party was effectively over as housing prices stalled around 2006, but the mortgage machine continued using increasingly illicit practices. The actual collapse was finally obvious in 2008 with the bailout of Bear Stearns, but the actual crash came after the bankruptcy of Lehman Brothers (replacing WorldCom as the largest bankruptcy in American history) in October 2008. Credit markets froze up and it took the mammoth money machine of the Federal Reserve and the Troubled Asset Relief Program (TARP) federal equity investments to salvage the financial system. Even with the massive government effort, the deepest post–World War II recession was on—called the *Great Recession*. The DOW fell from 14,164 in October 2007 to a low of 6,594 (down 53.4 percent) in March 2009.

Despite the finance industry almost causing the collapse of the world-wide economy and a multi-trillion-dollar bailout of the *too-big-to-fail* banks, banking executives showed little if any remorse and no obvious shame come bonus time. After the failing Merrill Lynch was acquired by Bank of America (about the same time as the Lehman Brothers' bankruptcy), Merrill CEO John Thain paid out some $3.6 billion in bonuses but did not bother to tell B of A. The Treasury Department bailed out all the major banks by *buying* preferred stock and other equity instruments after they lost billions related to MBSs and other credit-related losses. Despite being in hock to the government, all still wanted to pay billions in so-called performance-based compensation.

Bad public relations followed *too-big-to-fail* financial CEOs testifying before Congress, defending their record and decisions in a seemingly arrogant style. For some reason, most people thought that after their disastrous behavior and government bailout the financial leaders would appear somewhat humble and perhaps apologize for their mistakes.

It was recognized that compensation incentives were a major cause of the Subprime Meltdown (the *Wall Street bonus culture*), and limiting executive pay became a priority for many in Congress. The Emergency Economic Stabilization Act of 2008, which provided TARP funding, limited the total compensation of the five top executives for firms receiving TARP funding upto $500,000, prohibited golden parachutes for this group, and capped earlier compensation payments of this group. The executives of these firms had the incentive to pay back the bailout money as soon as possible to return to massive compensation levels—and did. In 2009, American Insurance Group (AIG) was scheduled to pay a part of $450 million in *retention bonuses* in the unit responsible for issuing the infamous credit default swaps. Several bills were introduced in Congress to slap down AIG but none passed. In June 2009, the Treasury created the *Pay Czar* (Special Master) with authority over TARP recipients and responsibility for the compensation actually paid to the top 25 executives in each.

Given the gigantic financial scandal, Washington investigated and held hearings. President Obama planned a regulatory overhaul. A Financial Crisis Inquiry Commission was created to investigate. The House Financial Services Committee chaired by Barney Frank and the Senate Banking Committee chaired by Chris Dodd held hearings. The results were huge reports and the complex Dodd-Frank Financial Reform Bill of 2010. Not surprisingly, the Financial Crisis Inquiry Report issued in 2011 concluded that a systemic breakdown in accountability and ethics had occurred, and virtually all the players from home buyers and mortgage originators through the securitization pipeline to sellers and investors (and regulators) were responsible.

The Dodd-Frank Act of 2010, over 2,200 pages with 16 titles covering major aspects of reform, included a new Bureau of Consumer Protection, new over-the-counter (OTC) derivative requirements, and off-balance-sheet items. The bill included modest provisions on executive compensation. Financial firms (all of them, not just those receiving TARP funding) must disclose all incentive-based compensation to their federal regulators, and the bill essentially outlaws incentive plans deemed by the regulators as *too risky*. Executive clawback rules were expanded when financial statements were restated. Companies must disclose the ratio of CEO compensation to the median pay for all corporate employees. Most interesting is the *Say-on-Pay* provision, which requires a shareholder vote on executive compensation. However, the votes are nonbinding on the board. Most of the votes to date have been favorable, even among the TARP recipients.[32]

Median CEO pay (for the S&P 500) peaked in 2001 at $9.3 million and has been slightly down since. Compensation dropped after the tech collapse, rose again to $9.1 million at the top of the housing bubble, fell during the Great Recession, then rebounded since 2010. Despite two major scandals and recessions, CEOs did not give up much pay. Those at the very top have done remarkably well, with two CEOs receiving over $1 billion in 2012, Mark Zuckerberg of Facebook and Richard Kinder of Kinder Morgan.[33]

CHAPTER 5

Economic Theory

Explaining executive compensation: It's complicated.
—Kevin Murphy

Kevin Murphy may be the most respected economist focusing on executive compensation in America. He wrote a review article in 2012, in which the last section had the above title. His analysis showed that specific economic theories are incapable of explaining all the results to date (i.e., since the 1930s). Academic study of executive compensation has been ongoing in the United States at least since the 1930s when anecdotal evidence of perceived outrageous compensation at the top became widespread, followed by the accumulation of empirical data thanks to the Securities and Exchange Commission (SEC) and other government agencies.

Early studies tended to focus on firm size or performance to explain differences of executive compensation. Over the past 30 years, most economic-related analyses have been based on the agency theory and that will be the major focus of this chapter. The agency perspectives related to compensation are: (1) efficient contracting and (2) managerial power. In addition, "perceived costs" were introduced to explain the massive level of stock options granted in the 1990s. Selected academic research is summarized in Table 5.1.

Agency Theory

Precursors to agency theory go back to Adam Smith's *Wealth of Nations* and include a couple hundred years of further analysis.[1,2] However, the landmark study was Jensen and Meckling's 1976 article "Theory of the Firm," an attempt to explain ownership structure given property rights and finance, in addition to agency relationships. The fundamental

Table 5.1 Selected academic research[3]

Authors	Title	Year	Description
Adam Smith	The Wealth of Nations	1776	The start of classical economics, incorporating the importance of markets, laissez faire, the *invisible hand*, and the major factors of production (land, labor, and capital).
Jensen and Meckling	Theory of the firm: managerial behavior, agency costs and ownership structure	1976	Introduced agency theory to explain the importance of the corporation as a *nexus of contracts* and the relationship of principal and agent behavior.
Jensen and Murphy	Performance pay and top-management incentives	1990	Empirical analysis of CEO compensation, demonstrating that CEOs were *under-paid* based on performance and paid less (in real terms) than in the 1930s.
Jensen and Murphy	CEO incentives—It's not how much you make, but how	1990	Influential *Harvard Business Review* article claiming CEOs were paid like bureaucrats and compensation should be based on performance.
Yermack	Good timing: CEO stock option awards and company news announcements	1997	Early test of the managerial-power hypothesis, using option grant timing from the early 1990s. Options were typically granted before *favorable corporate news.*
Hall and Liebman	Are CEOs really paid like bureaucrats?	1998	Analysis challenges the Jensen and Murphy perspective. Focusing on *equity-at-stake* they find a strong relationship between firm performance and CEO compensation based on CEO holdings of stock and stock options.
Tosi, Werner, Katz, and Gomez-Mejia	How much does performance matter? A meta-analysis of CEO pay studies	2000	A meta-analysis of pay studies concluding that about 4% of CEO pay related to firm performance, versus 40% related to firm size. This result is consistent with the argument that CEOs are more interesting in growing the firm rather than maximizing profit—leading to more pay, power, and prestige, plus a size *premium.*

Piketty and Saez	*Income inequality in the United States, 1913–1998*	2003	The pay of high-income individuals (not just for executives) remained flat through the 1960, and increased after that. The authors viewed that as caused by *social norms*, which changed in the post–World War II period, including the impact of taxes.
Hall and Murphy	*The trouble with stock options*	2003	Described why options were the compensation of choice in the 1990s (saving cash, stock market euphoria), but the downsides became obvious with the tech crash (incentives for fraud, stock buybacks, but against dividends). Used the *perceived-cost* hypothesis to explain excess use of options during the 1990s. Restricted stock became preferred in the twenty-first century for executive compensation.
Bebchuk and Fried	*Pay without performance: the unfulfilled promise of executive compensation*	2004	Claimed that executive compensation was actually set by CEOs rather than an independent board; boards, especially at large firms, were weak. The rationale was that actual CEO pay packages are not consistent with optimal contracting principles (arm's length bargaining) and far outstripped compensation of other employees.
Lie	*On the timing of CEO stock option awards*	2005	Lie demonstrated the degree of *grant timing* that could only be explained by option backdating. SEC investigations (and convictions) followed.
Murphy and Zabojnik	*Managerial capital and the market for CEOs*	2007	Empirically tested the importance of outside hires of CEOs, which increased along with CEO compensation; the rationale was the increasing need for general managerial ability.
Efendi, Srivastava, and Swanson	*Why do corporate managers misstate financial statements? The role of option compensation and other factors*	2007	A multitude of financial restatements (typically associated with accounting manipulation and fraud) occurred after the tech crash, which were associated with large in-the-money stock option positions by the CEOs.

(*Continued*)

Table 5.1 Selected academic research[3] (Continued)

Authors	Title	Year	Description
Edmans and Gabaix	*Is CEO pay really inefficient? A survey of new optimal contracting theories*	2009	Survey article supporting efficient contracting, focusing on the importance of firm size and complexity. Large firms are more complex to run and CEOs with appropriate talent required greater compensation. Managerial talent is transferable and CEOs must be compensated in job-switching circumstances.
Frydman and Saks	*Executive compensation: a new view from a long-term perspective, 1936–2005*	2010	An empirical analysis over a 70-year period (subject to substantial data limitations), a long view demonstrating that executive compensation was flat for roughly 40 years and greatly increased after that; thus, economic rationales such as firm growth and pay-for-performance worked well only in the later period.
Frydman and Jenter	*CEO compensation*	2010	Survey article suggesting that both efficient contracting and managerial power were determinants of CEO compensation, but neither provided a complete analysis. Partial explanations included changing firm characteristics including firm growth, industry competition, and changing regulations.
Murphy and Sandino	*Executive pay and independent compensation consultants*	2010	Conflicts of interests involving compensation consultants include cross-selling services and satisfying CEOs to get repeat business. CEO compensation was higher in firms that used consultants, especially when they also provided other services to the corporations.
Armstrong, Jagolinzer, and Larcker	*CEO equity incentives and accounting irregularities*	2010	Empirical comparison of CEO equity incentives to three measures of accounting manipulation (restatements, class action lawsuits, and AAERs), showing no significance between CEO pay and manipulation.
Murphy	*The politics of pay: a legislative history of executive compensation*	2011	A review of Congressional legislation, regulations by the SEC and other agencies, accounting policies, and the impact on actual executive compensation. A major conclusion was that compensation follows regulation, while alternative economic theories struggle to explain the results.

Murphy	*Executive compensation: where we are, and how we got there*	2012	Survey article from one of the major researchers on executive compensation, including a theoretical overview, history, short review of the academic literature, and attempt to develop a *general theory*.
Pepper and Gore	*Behavioral agency theory: new foundations for theorizing about executive compensation*	2012	Thought piece suggesting that agency theory should be expanded from *classical economic theory* to incorporate behavioral economics. This better describes risk preferences of the major actors, as well as the limitations of rationality and information.
Van Essen, Heugens, Otten, and van Oosterhout	*An institution-based view of executive compensation: a multilevel meta-analytic test*	2012	Survey article (using meta-analysis) of over 300 studies across 29 countries; results modestly support optimal contracting, but with substantial variability across countries. However, an institutional framework is needed to account for cross-country differences.
Brookman and Thistle	*Managerial compensation: luck skill or labor markets?*	2013	In this empirical analysis of the reasons determining the variability of executive compensation, the authors show that management skills and labor market opportunities are important (as is firm size), while luck is insignificant.
Piketty	*Capital in the twenty-first century*	2014	Focused on income inequality with data from 1700–2010. Before the French Revolution the top 10% owned 90% of the wealth and the vast wealth differentials continued into the 20th century. The wealth differential collapsed in World War I and did not begin to return until the 1970s. The major factor in the U.S. was executive compensation. His recommended solution was a wealth tax and greater focus on education and other public policy reforms.

concept was the corporation as a nexus (or network) of contracts and, presumably, corporations are extremely efficient at writing and fulfilling contracts. Accordingly:

> We define an agency relationship as a contract under which one or more persons (the principal(s)) engage another person (the agent) to perform some service on their behalf which involves delegating some decision making authority to the agent. If both parties are utility maximizers there is good reason to believe that the agent will not always act in the best interests of the principal. The principal can limit divergences from his interest by establishing appropriate incentives for the agent and by incurring monitoring costs designed to limit the aberrant activities of the agent. ... However, it is generally impossible for the principal or the agent at zero cost to ensure that the agent will make optimal decisions from the principal's viewpoint.[4]

Agency theory and empirical analyses used in economics, finance, and accounting typically are based specifically on the relationship of the stockholders as principals (with the board of directors sometimes serving as a surrogate for the shareholders) and executives (often concentrating on the chief executive officer or CEO) as the agent. The focus on efficient contracting requires the analysis of transaction costs, various agency costs, and the need for monitoring. Corporations attempt to maximize profit and are assumed to be risk neutral (because investors can diversify risk). Executives as agents are assumed to be rational; risk averse (with limited ability to diversify risk); and rent seeking (i.e., maximize their own well-being).

Because principals and agents have conflicts of interest, agency costs are expected. Jensen and Meckling define agency costs as the sum of "(1) the monitoring expenditures by the principal, (2) the bonding expenditures by the agent, and (3) the residual loss,"[5] which represent wealth reduction to the shareholders. Three interrelated factors are associated with agency costs: moral hazard, adverse selection, and information asymmetry.

Information asymmetry means that one party has more information than the other; it is almost always assumed that the executive as agent has the information advantage and would act in the best interests of the agent but not the principal. Moral hazard means that the agents are willing to take risks because they do not take full responsibility for their actions or are insulated from the repercussions.[6] Adverse selection is a decision with unexpected or undesired results generally because of information asymmetries.

Principals are expected to write contracts to reduce agency costs. Monitoring can be used to reduce information asymmetries and limit moral hazard. Accounting techniques include financial audits, detailed financial disclosure requirements, and various internal control systems. In addition, incentive contracts can be written to align executive incentives with those of the stockholders. These could include cash bonuses to encourage a focus on accounting earnings, sales, or both. Contracts can encourage ownership interests by executives including stock options, restricted stock, and so on. The greater the ownership stake, the more the interests of the principals, and agents should be aligned.

Jensen and Murphy

As previously described in Chapter 4, Jensen and Murphy's 1990 article in *Harvard Business Review* seemed to set the gears in motion for corporations to load executives up on stock options plus other forms of stock ownership and regulators to encourage performance-based pay. In a second 1990 article entitled "Performance Pay and Top-Management Incentives," published in the *Journal of Political Economy*, Jensen and Murphy made a more detailed academic case. The focus was on models and empirical tests of optimal (efficient) contracting. Agency theory expectations predicted that executive compensation ties the CEO's (as an agent) expected utility to that of the shareholder. Because stockholders want to maximize wealth, CEO compensation should be based on changes in stockholder wealth.[7]

The empirical evidence of Jensen and Murphy was based on 2,213 CEOs from 1974 to 1986 representing 1,295 large public corporations (data available from *Forbes* Executive Compensation Surveys). Because of data limitations, results were based on fewer CEO-years (or various subsamples).[8] The period under study represented a transition period before the "great explosion" of the 1990s.

The Jensen and Murphy focus was on performance-based compensation and stock ownership, which (according to their view of agency theory) would provide the best incentives for the CEOs to work in the interests of stockholders. They used a model of "pay-performance sensitivity," defined as the dollar change in CEO wealth relative to the dollar change in shareholder wealth (based on total market value of the corporation). The findings showed a positive and significant relationship, but small. Salary-plus-bonus showed a pay-performance elasticity of little more than 0.1 percent; that is, a $1,000 increase in the shareholder value resulted in an average $0.0135 increase in salary-plus-bonuses. Their measure of total compensation (which did not include stock options) implied a pay-performance of 0.33 percent, an increase in CEO compensation of $0.033 for every $1,000 increase in shareholder value.

Jensen and Murphy did further analysis of stock options (not available in the *Forbes* data) and total stock holdings based on a much smaller sample of 79 large *Fortune* 500 manufacturing firms, which suggested a much larger increase in CEO compensation; $0.145 per $1,000 increase in shareholder value based on options and $0.33 for total compensation.

Back to the *Forbes* data, the median CEO held 0.25 percent of the corporation's stock in 1987, with a value of about $3.5 million. Because of skewness, the mean value was 2.4 percent and $41 million. CEOs at smaller firms held larger percentages of stock, but with lower valuations (a median value of $2.6 million versus $4.7 million at larger firms).

Jensen and Murphy demonstrated that CEOs' salary and bonuses were associated with accounting, earnings and sales, with compensation rising $0.177 per $1,000 change in annual income. An analysis by the Conference Board in the mid-1980s indicated that over 90 percent of large manufacturing firms had bonus plans and the average bonus was about 50 percent of base salary. Consequently, the strong findings related to accounting earnings were not surprising.

Jensen and Murphy attempted to analyze the impact of poor performance on terminations, on the assumption that the impact should be negative—poor performance should lead to higher termination rates and reduced compensation. In fact, apparent termination at poor performers did happen, but infrequently.[9] However, poor performance did lead to lower compensation and the termination potential increased. The average wealth loss for a CEO about 46 years old was estimated at $510,000 and a turnover probability of 3.6 percent when the firms earned a 0 percent return in the previous two years relative to the market. The calculations related to poor performance were complex, but the interpretation was that poor performance is associated with a wealth loss and a rising termination potential but with small magnitudes.

Jensen and Murphy also compared their data from the 1970s to 1980s with data available from a 1940 Work Projects Administration (WPA) survey for 1934 to 1938. The data looked at the highest-paid executive of 748 large companies, over half of which were listed on the New York Stock Exchange (NYSE). Using constant (1986) dollars, the salaries-plus-bonuses for executives of the 1930s were higher than those of the Jensen and Murphy sample, with mean pay of $813,000 (1934 to 1938) versus $645,000 (1974 to 1986) for the top 25 percent largest firms. Median pay was closer, $639,000 versus $607,000. The salaries-plus-bonuses relative to corporate market value also were higher for the 1930s period, 0.11 percent versus 0.034 percent.

A key point to the Jensen and Murphy analysis was: "The incentives generated by CEO stock ownership have also declined substantially over the past 50 years.... CEO percentage of ownership in the largest 120 firms fell from a median of 0.30 percent in 1938 to 0.05 percent in 1974 and fell further to 0.03 percent in 1984."[10] From an efficient contracting view, the CEO incentives to act in the best interests were weak, suggesting executive behavior not in the best interests of the stockholders.

These Jensen and Murphy results tied back into the Jensen and Murphy *Harvard Business Review* warning that "CEOs were paid like bureaucrats," described in Chapter 4. This led to their influential recommendation that CEOs should be paid for performance based on "pay-performance sensitivity." The results were favorable legislation and regulation, plus an explosion in executive stock options and other performance-pay incentives. Simultaneously, there was an explosion in agency research on options and overall executive compensation. Because of seemingly unlimited data (thanks largely to SEC disclosure requirements) and a dynamic environment, multiple theoretical structures were developed and tested. Results for efficient contracting held up under limited circumstances, but were seldom generalizable.

Stock Options

Executive compensation more than tripled in real terms from 1992 to 2001. Median total compensation for S&P 500 CEOs in 2011 dollars rose from $2.9 million to $9.3 million (an average annual increase of 15.7 percent).[11] Most of this increase in compensation came from stock options.[12,13] As described in Chapter 4, the major reasons were the unintended consequences of regulations and other government actions. Academics soon attempted to explain the rise, primarily based on agency theory. The major focus was either on managerial power or efficient contracting, with some additional attention to the "perceived cost" of stock options.

"The 'efficient contracting' camp maintained that the observed level and composition of compensation reflects a competitive equilibrium in the market for managerial talent, and that incentives are structured to optimize firm value."[14] A key point is explaining the rise in stock options during the 1990s, generally based on the executive incentives to act in the best interests of stockholders. Various efficient contract approaches were tested. One approach was the higher cost of hiring outside CEOs, focusing on the importance of "general managerial capital."[15] An alternative model focused on the importance of firm size and market capitalization. Market cap expanded exponentially during the 1990s and CEO pay correlated almost perfectly with the rise in market cap over the decade.[16] Various studies showed that stock prices rose when corporations announced long-term compensation plans, and CEO compensation was higher in firms that performed well (presumably because of better management talent).

Managerial power is an alternative explanation for the rise in options, essentially self-interested executives' excess compensation from unknown stockholders. Options were preferable to cash because options are less transparent and their hidden costs served as a method to camouflage management's rent-seeking behavior. CEOs rely on *captive board members* catering to the powerful CEOs. "CEOs extract rents from shareholders by timing their option grants to occur just before the release of good news,[17] by insider trading through their family charitable foundations,[18] through lucrative severance and change in control provisions,[19,20] and by consuming excessive perquisites."[21,22]

A third potential explanation for explosive option granting is the perceived-cost hypothesis; decisions are made based on the accounting of options as *costless* (no compensation expense had to be recorded for options) rather than the *real* or *economic cost*. The real cost can be measured (e.g., using Black-Scholes) and options dilute (increase) outstanding shares. The *near-costless compensation* argument, according to this theory, explains why options were issued in vast quantities during the 1990s.

Empirical Research

Beginning with Jensen and Murphy[23] empirical compensation research used agency models to analyze total compensation, compensation components, and the relationship of compensation to various measures of performance and other firm-specific factors. The original point of Jensen and Murphy's pair of 1990 articles was to demonstrate that executive pay was not based on economic performance but should be. This led to tests of the alternative hypotheses developed under agency theory and different interpretations of results.

Research on the 1990s' Compensation Explosion

Yermack[24] was one of the first to use the managerial-power hypothesis to explain the timing of CEO option grants. He looked at 620 options awarded at Fortune 500 companies from 1992 to 1994, stating: "I find that the timing of awards coincides with favorable movements in company stock prices."[25] The ability to time option grant dates to generate large abnormal stock returns could best be explained by assuming that CEOs used their own power to determine the terms of their compensation. At that time, many CEOs served on their own compensation committees.

Hall and Liebman[26] challenged the Jensen and Murphy perspective of small compensation gains for corporation performance, claiming that they, in fact, are not *paid like bureaucrats*. Focusing on *equity-at-stake*, they find a strong relationship between firm performance and CEO compensation based on CEO holdings of stock and stock options. The difference in perspectives is key. Hall and Liebman claimed that CEOs at large corporations held relatively small percentages of stock (and options), but large dollar amounts that increased their *equity-at-stake incentives*. Thus, "The fortunes of CEOs are strongly related to the fortunes of the companies they manage."[27]

According to Hall and Murphy[28] companies find options useful because they can attract employees without using cash. No compensation expense needed to be recorded. Stock market euphoria during the 1990s seemed another reason for the interest in options. In addition, because of vesting, options have retention incentives for executives and other key employees. However, they are inefficient to most employees because they cannot be sold nor can they be diversified. Hall and Murphy found that employees valued options about half the market price as determined by Black-Scholes.[29] Hall and Murphy's was one of the first papers to propose the *perceived-cost* hypothesis, acknowledged by practitioners but dismissed by economists as suboptimal:[30] "The root of the trouble with options, we believe, is that decisions to grant such options are based on a perceived cost of options that is substantially lower than the economic cost."[31]

Murphy and Zabojnik[32] investigated the importance of external hires of CEOs to explain rising compensation consistent with efficient contracting, based on *Forbes* annual surveys showing 2,783 CEOs appointed at 1,323 companies from 1970 to 2005. External hires rose from 15 percent in the 1970s, to 26 percent in the 1990s, and 32.7 percent from 2000 to 2005. The hypothesis was that general managerial ability was increasingly important rather than *firm-specific* talent at major corporations. For example, more CEOs had MBA degrees (which doubled to 28.7 percent over the period), a larger percent of which were external hires. They found CEO pay higher for outsiders (15 percent higher on average) and in industries where outside hiring was common, a major factor why CEO salaries tripled in real terms over their period of study.

A survey article by Frydman and Jetner[33] attempts to explain that both efficient contracting and managerial power are partial explanation of compensation, especially during the 1990s. This is partly because certain finding can be interpreted under either approach. CEO compensation tracked increases in market value, other measures of firm size, and performance. Various explanations of managerial talent in increasingly competitive industries exist and moral hazard problems rise as corporations get bigger.

For example, rising CEO pay could be explained by board capture or greater monitoring and effectiveness by boards seeking better CEO talent (and willing to pay for it). One factor in the study by Frydman and Jetner that fits the managerial power hypothesis is *stealth compensation*, items such as perks and certain pension and severance benefits that can be hidden.

However, the results of the 1990s are not generalizable over longer periods. This view is reinforced by Frydman and Saks,[34] an empirical analysis over 70 years beginning in the 1930s demonstrating that specific results are time sensitive. The explanations for the 1990s results do not work at all for the first 40 or so years of the analysis (from the 1930s at least until the 1970s). Looking at long-term income (1913 to 1998), Piketty and Saez[35] hypothesized that changing social norms are an answer, as norms against income inequality weakened and CEOs were in the position to increase their own pay. A major factor was progressive income tax, with top rates staying above 90 percent until the 1960s, but dropping to 28 percent with the Tax Reform Act of 1986.

After the Tech Crash

Because options reward only stock-price appreciation, significant deficiencies in incentive structures became clear in the tech crash of 2000 to 2002. Many executives attempted to maintain stock prices at a high level through accounting manipulation and fraud. CEOs with options also had incentives to favor share repurchases (treasury stock) and avoid dividends.[36] The discovery of fraud often led to bankruptcy, as at Enron and WorldCom.

Beginning at least with Jensen and Murphy,[37] experts have recommended that executive pay be linked with economic performance. A major argument was between those arguing that executives deserved the high pay (the *worth every nickel* argument, consistent with efficient contracting) versus those finding no basis for compensation relative to performance (the *no rational basis* argument, consistent with managerial power).[38] A meta-analysis by Tosi et al.[39] concluded that less than 5 percent of CEO compensation was based on firm performance. On the other hand, firm size could explain 40 percent of compensation, consistent with the argument of a *size premium*. Tosi et al. used factor analysis to convert the variable used by various studies to (1) firm performance (based on 30 variables) and (2) firm size (16 variables).

The academic analysis of manipulation incentives of executives followed the tech crash. Efendi et al.[40] documented the relationship of stock option holdings of the CEO with evidence of accounting abuse. They looked at financial restatements[41] as a measure of misleading or misstated financial statements. The in-the-money options (the stock price was higher than the exercise price of the options) of the CEO[42] was the incentive measure used (as a measure of overvalued stock) to justify accounting manipulation or fraud. A multivariate analysis showed that the amount of CEOs' in-the-money options was the most influencing factor for restatements. CEOs had an average of over $50 million in options value, versus $8.9 million at non-restatement firms.

A number of other studies also looked at the relationship of CEO equity incentives and various definitions of accounting manipulation and fraud, with mixed results. Most found a positive relationship similar to that by Efendi et al., but not all. For example, Armstrong et al.[43] tested *high-powered equity incentives* as measured by portfolio delta, defined as the change in the CEO's equity portfolio for a 1 percent change in the company's stock price for the period 2001 to 2005 (roughly the post-tech bust period).[44] The three manipulation measures used were (1) financial restatements, (2) class action lawsuits related to accounting misrepresentations, and (3) Accounting and Auditing Enforcement Releases (AAERs) based on an investigation of accounting manipulation by the SEC. The empirical results showed no significant relationship between manipulation and CEO incentives. On the other hand, Armstrong et al. pointed out: "modest evidence consistent with the alternative explanation that equity incentives align managers' interests with those of shareholders."[45]

Hall and Murphy stated the advantages of restricted stock rather than options in providing incentives to CEOs and other top executives. First, holders have essentially identical incentives as stockholders (and are not limited to stock appreciation). CEOs holding out-of-the-money options have incentives to invest in risky ventures, while restricted stockholders do not. S&P 500 companies granted options worth an average of $238 million in 2000, but only $141 million in 2002.[46] Corporations have been increasing restricted stock and reducing options ever since.

The discovery of options backdating and spring loading early in the twenty-first century provided further evidence of managerial power. In backdating, the grant date is set at an earlier date, typically when the stock price is at its lowest of the period, increasing the overall gain to the holder (a potentially illegal act, which reduces the cash collected by the company when the options are exercised). Spring loading occurs when companies award options just before good news is announced, expecting to boost stock price. Yermack[47] found that stock prices rose after the option grant date, but it was Erik Lie who discovered the extraordinary degree of *grant timing* that could only be explained by opportunistic behavior.[48]

One additional group to blame for high executive pay is executive compensation consultants, a group investigated by both the SEC and Congress. As a result, in 2009, the SEC expanded its disclosure rules, requiring corporations to disclose fees paid to compensation consultants in some circumstances and (as part of the Dodd-Frank bill), any conflicts of interest raised by the consultants. As pointed out by Murphy and Sandino: "Critics of perceived abuses in executive pay have increasingly accused the consultants as being complicit in the alleged excesses in compensation."[49]

Murphy and Sandino[50] investigate the potential conflicts of interest for compensation based on CEO compensation for 1,046 U.S. corporations in 2006 (plus supplementary analysis of 124 Canadian companies).[51] They found that the CEO compensation was 13 percent higher when the consultants worked exclusively for the compensation committee of the board. In addition, U.S. CEO salaries were 18 percent higher when the compensation consultants provided other services to the corporation (and also higher for Canadian firms).

Murphy investigated CEO pay for the S&P 500 from 2001 to 2011.[52] The top median pay in 2001 was at $9.3 million, which dropped in 2002 to $8.1 million during the tech bust, recovered in 2006 to $9.1 million, then dropped during the subprime crisis and rose to $9.0 million in 2011. Murphy called this "the first prolonged stagnation in CEO pay since the early 1970s."[53] Significantly, the major pay category was option in 2001, while restricted stock became the largest by 2011 (36 percent of total pay, up from 8 percent in 2001). Options dropped substantially, but remained a large pay category (from 53 percent to 21 percent).

Brookman and Thistle[54] investigated the relative importance of luck, management skill and labor market opportunities as determinants of executive's total compensation. They looked at over 28,000 executives from almost 2,800 firms from 1993 to 2008. Median compensation was $972,000 (compared to over $2.4 million for those with the title chairman and CEO). Luck was measured as the firm's stock return performance relative to the average industry performance; outside labor market opportunities were based on relative compensation across the industry, and management skill was based on a complex model of management characteristics. Their results show that management skills were the most important determinant of pay (explaining 40 percent of executive pay variability), followed by labor market opportunities. Firm size was also significant as a control variable. Luck was not significant. They view the results as consistent with the importance of executive human capital skills that are transferable across firms.[55]

Expanded Analysis: Psychology and Behavioral Economics

Traditional economic models assume that all the actors are rational, markets are efficient, and the future can be forecast without bias. Psychologists have challenged these assumptions for decades, and behavioral economics attempts to more realistically model actor and market behavior. Most academic fields of business (including accounting, finance, and management) have incorporated these (at least to a limited extent) in empirical research, including executive compensation issues, such as Pepper and Gore.[56] A key point is that executive behavior is not fully rational, because of factors such as optimism, overconfidence, and various managerial biases. Because of bounded rationality, for example, managers often use (presumably suboptimal) heuristics (rules of thumb). Larkin et al. argue that "predictions of agency theory often fail because performance-based pay is less effective than the theory predicts,"[57] caused in part by behavioral biases.

One approach is to modify agency models to include behavioral elements to explain results appearing contradictory or unexplainable based on the traditional agency theory. Pepper and Gore[58] added behavioral assumptions about executive motivation beyond the strict focus on compensation (including intrinsic motivation—internally generated satisfaction), modifications to risk and uncertainly, and assumed that agents are more loss averse (prefer avoiding losses relative to acquiring gains) rather than risk averse. Mishina et al.[59] considered behavioral traits that encourage illegal acts. They found that loss aversion, executive hubris, and *house money effects* (prior gains increase risk seeking) were associated with firms with a higher propensity to commit illegal acts.

Baker and Wurgler[60] describe manager biases associated with behavioral finance. Overconfidence, a common behavior attribute, is more likely in an executive setting because situations can be complex, making it difficult to demonstrate faulty analysis and decision making. Overconfidence can result in additional risk taking; those performing well (and their superiors) assume that this is because of extraordinary ability. The literature includes hubris-based mergers, where acquisitions are common but a large percentage fails. Contracts rely on reference points to compare relative performance. Satisfaction should be based on performance measures above reference points (such as measure of earnings per share).[61]

The application of agency theory to executive pay is based on extrinsic motivation, particularly *pay-for-performance*. Behavioral approaches, on the other hand, consider both intrinsic (self-determined) and extrinsic (externally determined) motivations, a topic covered by Rebitzer and Taylor[62] (2011). Intrinsic motivations include the concept of *a calling*, a dedication to the job (such as advocacy, certain types of education, and so on). This calling could include an executive in various high-tech fields. While high pay or *a competitive market* could encourage executives who consider their careers only a job, low pay may encourage those to whom the job is a vocation or calling. Of course, in many cases, monetary incentives can crowd out any intrinsic motivations.[63]

CHAPTER 6

International Comparisons

*One of the most widely accepted stylized facts in the executive compen-
sation literature is that chief executive officers (CEOs) in the United
States are paid significantly more than their foreign counterparts.*
—Nuno Fernandes, Miguel Ferreira, Pedro Matos,
and Kevin Murphy

Executive compensation in the United States may be outrageous by
any measure, including the relative compensation paid in other countries. Descriptive comparisons seem to bear this out, but as with the last
chapter, it is still complicated. The first problem is comparable data. U.S.
generally accepted accounting principles (GAAP) and disclosure rules are
based on accounting standards set by the Financial Accounting Standards
Board (FASB) (plus predecessor bodies) and the Securities and Exchange
Commission (SEC). Most corporations in foreign countries are based on
International Financial Reporting Standards (IFRS), which differ from
U.S. GAAP. In addition, while the SEC has required compensation disclosure of top executives since the 1930s, comparable disclosure standards
in most major countries started in the twenty-first century.

Comparable descriptive data come from Fernandes et al.[1] for major
U.S. corporations and those of 13 other developed countries for 2006,
which are summarized in Figure 6.1. Data come from 1,648 U.S. companies and 1,251 non-U.S. firms. The number of corporations by country
range from six for South Africa to 561 for UK. U.S. average total compensation was $5.5 million (median pay: $3.3 million), compared to the
non-U.S. pay of $2.8 million (median: $1.6 million). Thus, without any
adjustments or other considerations, U.S. chief executive officers (CEOs)
made, on average, almost twice that of their foreign counterparts.[2] An
important consideration is the composition of pay, from straight salary to equity-based compensation. Corporations in all countries used

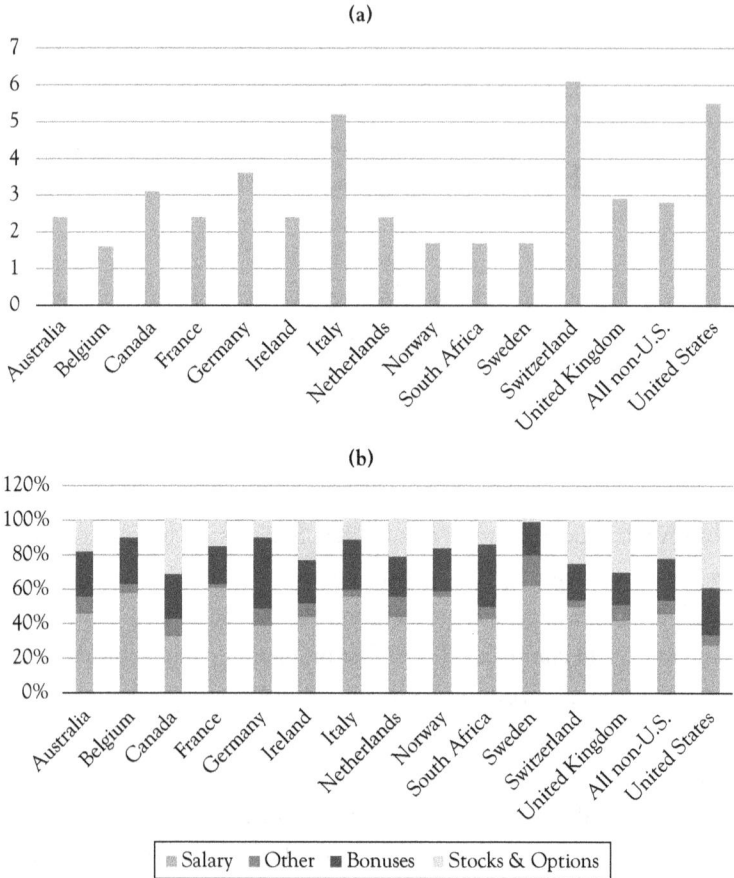

Figure 6.1 CEO compensation across 14 developed countries (2006)
(a) mean CEO total pay ($ millions) and (b) CEO compensation
percent. CEO, chief executive officer

Source: Adapted from Fernandes et al. (2013), Table 1, p. 328.

equity-based compensation (stock and options), but U.S. firms paid the
most, 39 percent of total compensation. Canadian and British firms also
had equity compensation over 30 percent of total pay. U.S. firms paid only
28 percent of total compensation as cash salary, plus a hefty 27 percent
in bonuses; thus, most compensation was in the form of (riskier) performance-based pay. Non-U.S. firms paid an average 46 percent salary and
24 percent bonuses, leaving stock and options at only 22 percent.

Why did U.S. firms pay CEOs more than foreign counterparts?
Fernandes et al.[3] show that for a variety of reasons, the differences are

modest based on a detailed empirical analysis, at least for 2006 (but not necessarily earlier). There are different legal structures, corporate cultures, and governance that presumably result in pay differences. In addition, there are the gigantic global firms (such as Royal Dutch Shell versus Exxon Mobil, Toyota versus General Motors). Are there pay differences for the giant foreign-domiciled firms? These are issues discussed in this chapter.

International Accounting and Disclosure

GAAP in the United States is strictly a domestic matter. Firms anywhere else in the world have different accounting and reporting standards.[4] Historically, GAAP varied substantially. U.S. standards were considered rules based, while other countries were more principles based.[5] The predecessor of the International Accounting Standards Board (IASB) was created in 1973 (the same time as the FASB) to develop global accounting standards, now called IFRS. Countries around the world gradually shifted to IFRS. Disclosures of executive compensation, on the other hand, have developed country by country. The United States was the first, followed after a long interval by the United Kingdom and Canada and, eventually, most of the remaining developed countries.

International Financial Reporting Standards

Following calls for global accounting standards from the 1960s, the International Accounting Standards Committee (IASC) was established in 1973 primarily to help harmonize the financial accounting of the various countries of what became the European Union (EU).[6] The IASC issued International Accounting Standards from 1973 through 2001 (some 41 of them). It was reorganized in 2001 as the IASB, which issues IFRS (14 through 2014). Although relatively few countries adopted international standards during the twentieth century, by 2009, the EU and over 100 other countries adopted IFRS and the number continues to rise.

Countries (and their accountants) have been reluctant to give up sovereignty over accounting and reporting—based both on specific judgment and principles, as well as political considerations. The EU adopted IFRS for all European companies trading on the regulated European markets, beginning in 2005. South Africa required companies listed on the Johannesburg Stock Exchange to follow IFRS also beginning in 2005. Canada permitted *publicly accountable enterprises* to adopt IFRS beginning in 2011.

The FASB (and to a lesser extent the SEC) has worked for decades to establish joint standards that converge with IFRS. This effort has run hot and cold over the years as board members and attitudes changed. Many experts felt that U.S. GAAP were superior and not enthusiastic to compromise, while others believed that universal accounting standards around the world are essential to a global economy. To date, standards have moved closer. For example, the FASB now requires stock options to be recorded on the income statement based on options pricing models, consistent with IFRS.

U.S. GAAP remain different from IFRS. In addition, data before 2005 for European countries differed by country, and in Canada and other non-European countries the differences have various dates. Consequently, data analysis is hampered by these differences. This is particularly true of executive compensation, disclosure of which has been widely available in the United States since the 1930s, but available fairly recently in other countries (and the amount of disclosure also varies).

In general, U.S. GAAP and IFRS are similar on most issues directly related to compensation accounting, in part because of the process of harmonization. Both passed similar standards in 2004 related to stock options. Statement of Financial Accounting Standards (SFAS) 123R required the expensing of options when granted. IFRS 2, *Share-based Payment*, had similar requirements. There are technical differences on pension accounting, but standards are similar. International Accounting Standard (IAS) 19 on *Employee Benefits* also includes some technical differences with U.S. GAAP, such as the calculation of past service cost, the discount rates to be used, and pension asset gains and losses.

Institutional Perspective

An alternative approach to agency theory when dealing with international comparisons is an institutional perspective, because business strategies, practices, and outcomes are based on country-level institutional factors.

These factors include the country's legal system and related characteristics, investor protection laws, various informal factors such as the relative power of labor organizations, political differences and powers, and their influence on business, various *soft rules* that can define ethical and proper behavior or encourage various types of ownership concentrations, and watchdog organizations (including the media).[7]

Formal institutions take on multiple forms, such as common law versus civil law, tax policies, corporate ownership structures, and other legal requirements. The formal institutional framework provides structure and incentives for economic and financial development. Important requirements for executive compensation are investment protection laws. Disclosure rules can benefit (or hinder) investors relative to executives, beginning with disclosing compensation practices and actual pay of specific top executives. In addition, laws may deal harshly (or not) with self-benefiting actions by management such as claw backs and criminal prosecutions. The rights of employees and creditors differ across countries. When labor unions, for example, have considerable power (including seats on the board of directors), executive pay is more likely to be constrained.

Institutions also include informal customs and cultural patterns beyond formal institutions, such as how labor unions function is a specific organization or *implied rules* of social responsibility or corporate governance. The roles of banks and various institutional investors can be based on culture rather than legal requirements. The same may be true of watchdog organizations. Informal institutions may be more difficult to evaluate empirically.

Executive Compensation Disclosures by the 1990s and Initial Comparisons

Despite IFRS, the disclosure of CEO and other top executive compensation has been country based and, similar to the U.S. experience, expanded after public or political outrage over compensation, severance packages, and other issues of CEOs. Related issues were the use of various tax incentives (or disincentives) and other regulations designed for economic policy reasons rather than raising taxes. Also, just as the United States turned more conservative with the *Reagan Revolution*, so did a number of European countries. Britain is particularly interesting on all three of these points.

Margaret Thatcher became prime minister of the United Kingdom in 1979 and served until 1990, actually leading Reagan in the *conservative revolution*. Privatization of state-owned companies and deregulation followed. Tax-advantaged options became part of the reform package and, for a time, most UK firms issued employee options (up from virtually zero in 1979). Top executives receiving options were taxed at the capital gains rate (if the shares were sold after being exercised).

Thatcher's government privatized Britain utilities, allowing executives to receive options (conveniently taxable at the capital gains rate). Unfortunately, the exercise prices substantially understated market value, allowing the executives' windfall gains when the options vested. At the same time, customers saw much higher utility rates. The result was the Greenbury Committee Report of 1995 calling for changing tax rules, changes in stock options (e.g., recommending taxing options at the ordinary income rate and increasing emphasis on performance-based options), and expanding disclosure rules for executives. The use of options fell in the United Kingdom, while exploding in the United States in the mid-to-late 1990s.

Thanks to the new disclosure rules, UK compensation for specific CEOs could be compared to U.S. counterparts for the first time.[8] This was done by Conyon and Murphy,[9] comparing the CEO compensation of the 500 largest UK companies to the top 500 U.S. CEOs. The average British CEO made about $972,000 in total compensation for fiscal year 1997 (median salary was $683,000), while U.S. counterparts averaged $5.9 million (median of $2.5 million).[10] This was not a reasonable direct comparison, because U.S. firms were much larger, the composition of compensation differed, in addition to other differences. The results of Conyon and Murphy and other international research papers are summarized in Table 6.1.

As previously described, U.S. firms relied on buckets of stock options during the 1990s. UK firms relied mainly on base salary (59 percent of total pay), 18 percent cash bonus, options at 10 percent, restricted stock and other forms of long-term incentive plans of 9 percent, and various others at 5 percent. The U.S. equivalents were 29 percent, 17 percent,

Table 6.1 **Selected academic research**

Authors	Title	Year	Description
Conyon and Murphy	The prince and the pauper? CEO pay in the United States and United Kingdom	2000	The average U.K. CEO (based on the largest 510 corporations) total compensation was $972,000 in 1997, about one-sixth of U.S. pay for the top CEOs. When adjusted for firm size and industry, the U.S. premium was still 215% over U.K. counterparts.
Conyon and Schwalbach	Executive compensation: evidence from the UK and Germany	2000	Described executive compensation for the United Kingdom and Germany based on Towers Perrin survey data. Corporate governance differed between the two countries, with Germany having a two-tier management (full-time employees) and supervisory (outsiders). U.K. top executives (1993–1995) averaged $645,000, while German executives averaged only $330,000.
Zhou	CEO pay, firm size, and corporate performance: evidence from Canada	2000	Analyzed CEO compensation for 755 Canadian firms from 1991 to 1995. CEO total pay averaged $633,000, with salary about 75% of cash compensation and options, 40% of total compensation.
Conyon, Fernandes, Ferreira, Matos, and Murphy	The executive compensation controversy: a transatlantic analysis	2011	Overview of U.S. versus European executive compensation, including history, descriptive analysis, and empirical analysis for 2003–2008. Regression analysis indicated that the U.S. pay premium over European CEOs was small in 2008 (about 12%), down from a 58% premium in 2003.
Van Essen, Heugens, Otten, and Oosterhout	An institution-based view of executive compensation: a multi-level meta-analytic test	2012	Survey article of over 300 studies of executive compensation in 29 countries. Alternative theories evaluated were optimal contracting and institutional framework. The institutional perspective proved modestly positive for explaining executive compensation and firm performance.
Fernandes, Ferreira, Matos, and Murphy	Are U.S. CEOs paid more? New international evidence	2013	Empirical analysis for 2006 of 1,648 U.S. CEOs versus 1,251 non-U.S. CEOs. U.S. average total compensation was $5.5 million, while non-U.S. CEOs averaged $2.8 million. However, after controlling for firm characteristics, ownership structure, board structure, and relative risk composition of pay, the premium disappeared.

42 percent, 4 percent, and 8 percent, respectively. As expected, the major U.S. pay category was stock options at 42 percent. Unlike U.S. firms, British options were mainly performance based, vesting on specific performance criteria (U.S. options were more often time based). About the same number of firms paid cash bonuses (the United Kingdom at 81 percent versus 83 percent for U.S. corporations); however, 72 percent of U.S. firms gave options, versus 50 percent for UK firms.

Conyon and Murphy noted differences in equity holdings. UK CEOs averaged $11.6 million of share holdings (median: $759,000), while U.S. CEOs held almost $100 million (median $5.4 million). This amounted to 0.21 percent of the equivalent outstanding U.K. company shares and 1.6 percent of outstanding U.S. shares. Reinforcing the importance of equity-based pay (particularly options in the United States) was the difference in stock performance. The S&P 500 rose about 300 percent during the 1990s, while the UK equivalent (the Financial Times Stock Exchange or FTSE Index) rose about 150 percent. This almost certainly translated into the rising demand for options, especially in the United States.

An additional reason for pay differences was the combined CEO and chairman position. The combined position is expected to pay more for two reasons: (1) the CEO and chairman had additional responsibilities and (2) the person had more influence over both the board and compensation committee. About two-thirds of U.S. firms were run by CEOs and chairmen while only 18 percent of British firms combined the position. Conyon and Murphy estimated that the combined position paid on average 11 percent more at U.S. firms and 19 percent more at UK firms.

Conyon and Murphy used regression analysis to control for firm size, industry, and other factors to determine an average *U.S. pay premium*. After controlling for size and industry, they claimed a 47 percent pay premium for salary and bonuses and 215 percent more in total pay (versus the 366 percent overall difference based on median total salary, $2.5 million versus $683,000). One additional factor considered by Conyon and Murphy was culture: "The U.S. wage premiums for 'superstars' in all occupations persists in spite of the similarities in language, culture, tax regimes, and institutions."[11]

In 1993, all publicly traded companies in the Canadian province of Ontario were required to disclose top executive compensation based on the Ontario Securities Regulations. Most of the larger corporations were traded on the Toronto Stock Exchange. These firms, on average, were only about a tenth the size of U.S. firms and heavily weighted in energy and mining companies (almost 30 percent). Zhou[12] analyzed 755 of these firms for fiscal years 1993 to 1995. Total CEO compensation averaged $622,000 (with a median value of $392,000).[13] Salary averaged 75 percent of cash compensation, with bonuses 19 percent of cash compensation, and stock options about 40 percent of total compensation. Seventy-five percent of firms paid bonuses and 86 percent stock options. Larger firms, on average, paid higher percentages of both bonuses and options.

Conyon and Schwalback[14] described executive compensation for UK and German corporations based on Towers Perrin survey data, which were severely limited.[15] Substantial legal and economic differences existed between the two countries, which could partially explain compensation differences. Corporate governance differed between the two countries, with Germany having a two-tier management board (full-time employees) and a supervisory board (outsiders). The supervisory boards were composed of employee-elected members and stockholder-elected members. Major banks and other financial institutions controlled much of the stock, and about 10 percent of the stockholder board members were bank representatives. In addition, interlocking boards were common (a practice outlawed in America).

According to Conyon and Schwalbach, UK top executives (1993 to 1995) averaged $645,000 based on 102 companies, while German executives (48 companies) averaged only $330,000. Over the 1984 to 1996 period, UK executives had an annual 7.5 percent pay increase (salary plus bonus, in real terms), while German executives saw only a 1.4 percent increase. Data limitations made it difficult to draw many conclusions from this study beyond the legal and cultural differences of the two countries.[16]

Twenty-first Century Disclosures and Analysis

The twenty-first century saw two major meltdowns and recessions associated with massive manipulation and fraud. CEOs and other executives receiving huge options positions (especially those that vested only with substantial earnings or stock price growth requirements) had the incentives to manipulate revenues and earnings to meet earnings forecasts. The bankruptcies of Enron and WorldCom (in addition to many others) were the result of billion dollar frauds after years of manipulation, followed by mortgage manipulation of the financial industries and the near financial collapse of the entire world economy. One result was additional regulations in the United States and around the world as outrageous executive compensation was uncovered.

Vodafone (a British-based telecommunications multinational) acquired German-based Mannesman (a large telecom and manufacturing conglomerate) in a hostile takeover in 1999. The supervisory board of Mannesman approved some €60 million (about $67 million) in severance pay to the CEO and other top executives, after which both the CEO and board faced conspiracy and criminal charges. A similar case happened in France, where Elf (an oil company) was acquired by Totalfina (now Total, a multinational oil giant), also in 1999. Once again, the CEO received a massive severance package (worth €30 million).

Vivendi CEO Jean-Marie Messier turned a privatized French water utility into a mass media and telecom multinational. After a disastrous 2001, he was asked to resign—after he negotiated a €20 million severance package. He ultimately had to forego the pay after a lengthy court battle (and, interestingly, a SEC civil fraud case). More bad news on the French business front followed as Alstom (a power generation and transport conglomerate) fired CEO Pierre Bilger, after an embezzlement investigation and net losses (and finally a French government bailout in 2003). Despite this, Bilger was awarded a €4 million severance (which he eventually gave back). Similar stories occurred at Sweden's engineering firm ABB and oil giant Royal Dutch Shell (Britain and the Netherlands).[17]

The various countries involved in executive pay scandals conducted investigations and dealt with them in various ways, including increased disclosure requirements. Firms listed on the Irish Stock Exchange were required to disclose individual top executive pay in 2000. European firms cross-listed on U.S. and UK exchanges began to report executive compensation similar to the U.S. or UK rules. South Africa and Australia required executive pay disclosures beginning in 2000 and 2004, respectively. The EU recommended that all EU-listed companies report detailed individual compensation details beginning in 2003. By 2006, Belgium,

France, Germany, Italy, the Netherlands, and Sweden (all EU member) required (at least) CEO pay disclosures. Norway and Switzerland (not EU members) also required similar disclosures.[18]

By the mid-2000s, empirical data were available to compare CEO compensation of many developed countries to U.S. counterparts. Fernandes et al.[19] did exactly that (and is the source for Figure 6.1 comparisons), finding that U.S. CEOs in 2006 averaged almost double the total pay of non-U.S. CEOs ($5.5 million versus $2.8 million). Most of the article explained why the analysis must be adjusted to control for such factors as firm size, industry, ownership and board structure, and various CEO characteristics. Using regression analysis, they showed that U.S. CEO pay was (implied) to be 79 percent higher than other countries after adjusting for size and industry. However, when other controls are included, the pay premium drops to 31 percent. They were not done, because U.S. pay, which concentrates on stock options and other equity-based pay, is riskier than that of foreign counterparts. Risk-adjusted pay in their model was insignificantly higher for U.S. CEOs.[20]

Fernandes et al.[21] also analyzed CEO pay from 2003 through 2008. U.S. CEOs had a higher pay premium from 2003 through 2005 (108 percent, 109 percent, and 117 percent, respectively). After adjustments the U.S. pay premiums were still significant (36 percent, 32 percent, and 27 percent, respectively). Beginning in 2006, when the U.S. economy began to have financial difficulties, especially with mortgages and the housing boom (and U.S. corporations were required to expense stock options), the premium fell and the adjusted pay premium became insignificant from 2006 to 2008.[22] The claim was made by these and other economists that the U.S. focus on performance-based equity compensation is a more appropriate way to pay executives based on an agency framework.

Conyon et al.[23] compared CEO compensation of 1,425 large U.S. corporations to 892 corporations from nine European countries (all had revenues over €100 million, about $140 million). The average U.S. pay in 2008 was €3.7 million (median: €2.4 million), while European counterparts averaged €2.0 million (median: €1.2 million) or 53 percent of the U.S. average. The top pay category of U.S. CEOs was equity at 46 percent (29 percent for base salary), while the largest European category had a base salary at 50 percent (with equity pay at 19 percent). Base salary was similar for both groups, €557,000 for U.S. CEOs compared to €530,000 for Europeans. The major difference was in options and stock grants (€3.3 million versus €545,000). Echoing Jensen and Murphy, the authors claimed that European CEOs were still paid like bureaucrats. However, when total pay was controlled for firm, ownership, and board characteristics, the net U.S. pay premium fell to 12 percent (down from 108 percent in 2003).

Van Essen et al.[24] reviewed over 300 academic papers across some 29 counties to evaluate both an agency and institutional perspective. Their primary focus was the impact of executive pay contracts and firm performance. Overall, they found a modest but positive and significant relations between performance and compensation. This was particularly true for five countries: Finland, Germany, Israel, New Zealand, and Portugal. They concluded that: "Both formal institutions such as the rule of law and shareholder protections provisions and informal institutions such as ownership concentration and codes of good corporate governance help strengthen the relations between firm performance and executive pay."[25]

With data becoming available around the world during the twenty-first century, it became clear that U.S. executive pay (especially for CEOs) was substantially higher than that for foreign counterparts. The gap has dropped since 2002, thanks largely to institutional factors such as SFAS No. 123R and two major financial or economic collapses, but U.S. CEOs continued to have higher stock-based compensation. Agency modeling, however, suggested that much of the pay differential can be explained by size, industry, and various institutional and cultural factors as well as the risk differential associated with stock-based compensation. Noneconomists likely remain more skeptical about the relative significance of pay differentials.

CHAPTER 7

The Future of Executive Compensation

The reality is that executive pay is already heavily regulated on both sides of the Atlantic . . . . Our strong recommendation is to resist calls for further government regulation, and indeed governments should re-examine the efficacy of policies already in place.

—Martin Conyon, Nuno Fernandes, Miguel Ferreira, Pedro Matos, and Kevin Murphy

The history of executive compensation has been a complex gumbo of corporate and government actions that have changed the magnitudes and composition of pay over the last 80 years. For a variety of reasons from corporate greed to unintended consequences of government regulations, the system went from *bureaucratic* (according to Jensen and Murphy), through outrageous in the 1990s, to a modest pullback in the twenty-first century. Federal regulations continue (with the usual caveats of skepticism) as does the *traditional* view of economics and seemingly perverse incentives still available to executives. Is there hope of a reasonable system or will corporate America bounce around from one economic crisis to another driven by these perverse incentives?

The Bad News

In an earlier book, I described *The Economics of Bad Behavior*, not only the rationale for corporations to manipulate but virtually the requirement.[1] Since Adam Smith's *The Wealth of Nations* written in that eventful year 1776, and especially after the later neoclassical economic models, profit maximization became *de rigueur*. Traditional *economic man* is rational, selfish, and subject only to external motivation (mainly compensation). Economist Milton Friedman captured the libertarian view in his 1970 article, *The Social Responsibility of Business is to Increase its Profits*. The executive is the agent of the business and responsible for making as much money as possible. Government was responsible for limiting bad behavior, but, of course, deregulation was preferred by the libertarians and most of those subject to the regulations.

In addition to this economic perspective is the legal term *duty of loyalty*, requiring the board of directors and others to act in the best interests of the company and often interpreted as profit maximization. The interests of other stakeholders including customers, workers, and the public were not necessarily a concern. A famous court case to prove the point was the Dodge Brothers versus Ford Motor in 1919:

[Henry] Ford brazenly proclaimed that he was not managing Ford Motor Company to generate the best sustainable return for its stockholders. Rather, he announced that the stockholders should be content with the relatively small dividend they were getting and that Ford Motor Company would focus more on helping consumers by lowering prices and on bettering the lives of its workers and society at large by raising wages and creating more jobs.[2]

Ford lost. The court stated: "He could not subordinate the stockholders' best interest."[3] Presumably, every decision (whether ethical or not) should be based on a cost–benefit analysis. Perhaps, the most infamous case was the Ford Pinto of the 1970s. The car could burst into flames in a rear-end collision, caused by a gas tank not properly reinforced. The fix cost $11 per car. Ford projected the number of accidents, deaths, and injuries and compared that to the $11 times the millions of Pintos sold. The cost to fix the problem was deemed too great and no fix was made. Unfortunately, the cost–benefit memo came out in a court case and the ultimate legal liability proved vastly greater than the $11 a car fix. Similar problems by General Motors in a recent ignition switch case closely paralleled the Pinto experience.

Another disturbing development was the focus on quarterly earnings, the need to meet analysts expectation for earnings per share no matter what. For Enron (and hundreds of other, if less blatant, cases) that meant a growing list of fraudulent activities. Executive compensation at Enron and the rest reinforced the rabid obsession for *meeting or beating* analyst forecasts. After Enron, WorldCom, plus the subprime bubble, it should be clear that the corporate focus should be on the long term, three to five years out if not for the next decade or two. Unfortunately, the quarterly meet-or-beat fetish is still thriving at most corporations.

Lastly, executive compensation remains the prime motivator. Regulatory fixes are in, and corporations are changing compensation agreements. Statement of Financial Accounting Standards (SFAS) 123R became effective in 2006 requiring the expensing of options. Dodd-Frank requires a shareholder vote on compensation for the senior executives (although it is non-binding). Incentives are perhaps less blatant, although the focus is still on pay for performance and largely equity based. Restricted stock has replaced options as the major category. The basic environment seems basically unchanged as are the incentives to manipulate. Ultimately, it is still up to the board of directors of each individual corporation to determine what the *best interests* of the firm are.

Specific types of compensation behavior seem particularly egregious. First is the gigantic awards at some companies, $100 million plus a year or those that pay out a massive percent of annual net earnings as bonus compensation. Wall Street financial firms dominate here but have competition. A recent example was the compensation plan for Coca-Cola with a stock compensation plan for 2014 scheduled to pay potentially $13 billion to executives based on some 500 million equity awards (restricted stock plus options). Second is the huge pay at companies performing poorly. How can company compensation be performance based if all the normal dimensions of performance behave badly? Third is big termination awards for fired executives, where the stock price rises because the old chief executive officer (CEO) is out, such as the previously mentioned Robert Nardelli of Home Depot. Finally, large retention bonuses are paid to executives and other employees of failed companies, such as Enron, and the related bonuses paid at American Insurance Group (AIG) after its government bailout.

Recent experiences with the bursting of the tech bubble early this century and the subprime meltdown suggest flawed compensation as a contributing factor. The CEOs of banks with greater equity-based pay had the largest stock price losses during the Great Recession of 2008 to 2009, and banks receiving Troubled Asset Relief Program bailouts had the largest percentage drops in executive bonuses. This suggests that large (and presumably flawed) equity awards increase executive risk taking. On the other hand, other potentially perverse incentives like *too big to fail* may have been the primary cause.[4]

Good News Potential

All is not lost (or this may be wishful thinking on my part). The twenty-first century has seen many regulatory *fixes*. Executive compensation actually fell from their tech boom highs. Future culture will play a big role. It is not unreasonable that companies will focus on longer-term interests and performance, with only limited regard for quarterly earnings. In addition, the concept of social responsibility is part of the culture of at least some corporations. Regulatory changes continue and, it is hoped, reach toward the objectives of efficient and effective regulations in the public interest. Finally, the role of compensation changes over time.

Various regulations have been added (notably Sarbanes-Oxley and Dodd-Frank), attempting to reign in bad behavior. Sarbanes-Oxley, for example, beefed up corporate governance requirement and created a new audit regulator, the Public Company Accounting Oversight Board. Dodd-Frank addressed almost all the issues from the financial crisis of 2008 (although generating little optimism that the specific rules would solve the major financial problems). The effectiveness of regulations always is an open question. The head of the regulator makes a difference. Mary Jo White became the 31st chairman of the Securities and Exchange Commission (SEC) in 2013, with a reputation of competence, nonpartisanship, and success—a contrast to various predecessors and heads of other agencies. Sheila Bair (Chair of the Federal Deposit Insurance Corporation, 2006 to 2011) and Neil Barofsky (Special Inspector General in Charge of Oversight of the Troubled Asset Relief Program, 2008 to 2011) were other examples of regulatory heads considered effective (i.e., operating in the interests of the public). Leadership can make a difference to regulatory effectiveness, but regulatory leaders can change quickly—for good or bad.

Potentially quite important are the *say on pay* provisions of the Dodd-Frank Act. Investors vote on the executive compensation provisions of the corporation as part of the proxy statement vote. Although the vote is nonbinding, it certainly sends a signal of relative investor satisfaction on compensation. To date, the investors approved the pay packages at most corporations, possibly because the companies became more inclined to propose reasonable pay levels and explain the rationale in some detail.

Leadership also can come from the corporate sector. Amazon's CEO Jeff Bezos has a well-known long-term focus on market share rather than short-term profits, as do a number of other corporate heads—Warren Buffett comes to mind. Long-range planning determines the best strategies for current and future products and services, manufacturing techniques, marketing, customer satisfaction, and so on, all far removed from the fetish of quarterly earnings targets.

Many firms also have serious commitments to social or corporate responsibility (acting in the best interests of all stakeholders, including behaving ethically and improving the quality of life). Even the Business Roundtable (an organization promoting pro-business public policy) developed a *Statement on Corporate Responsibility* in the 1980s.[5] Chad Brooks of *Business News Daily* considered social responsibility a *reputational imperative*, with a large percent of consumers demanding this behavior.[6] It is no surprise that Ben & Jerry's and Whole Foods have major corporate responsibility commitments. However, many other major companies express an interest in social responsibility issues, including 3M, General Electric, Kellogg, PepsiCo, IBM, Cisco Systems, Ford, and Intel. *Major commitment* versus *marketing tool* is an open question, but it does indicate the increasing potential for a more honest corporate sector.[7]

Compensation contracting with CEOs and other executives can be more effective and appear *fairer*, promoting a much better match of pay to real corporate performance—a preferred corporate solution relative to additional regulations. Most recommended reforms call for a focus on long-term performance, usually emphasizing restricted stock, options, or other equity items. For example, a CEO incentive package may include a million options that vest in two years, have to be held two additional years after vesting before selling any shares and then may sell only 20 percent of the first year's award each year after that.[8] Given that executive compensation has declined slightly from the peak of 2001 to 2002, improved contracting may solve many of the problems with excess pay. Claw back provisions related to performance-based pay gone badly should be included.

APPENDIX 1

Microsoft Proxy Disclosures, 2013

Microsoft is one of America's largest companies and a tech giant. The corporation is a member of the Dow-Jones Industrial Average (DOW), with a market capitalization well over $300 billion. The purpose of the Microsoft Proxy Statement is to give stockholders the information they need to vote on key issues that are presented at the Annual Meeting; in the case of Microsoft specifically, the four proposals presented in Table A1.1 (All the disclosures specifically from the Proxy Statement are listed as tables and presented in the same order as in the Proxy.) The focus in this appendix is executive compensation and proposals two and three specifically relate to executive compensation issues, *say on pay* and performance criteria. The complete proxy statement is available for download from Microsoft's webpage. The top executive summary compensation table for Microsoft was shown in Chapter 1. However, it only shows up toward the end of the Proxy Statement, page 48 out of 53 pages. Considerable valuable information is presented that directly (and indirectly) relates to executive pay.

Important, if somewhat indirect to executive pay, is information on the board. All Microsoft board members must be elected each year. Microsoft had a relatively small board with the nine members listed in Table A1.2, two of whom (22 percent) are insiders, while the remaining seven are independent. Board membership is listed including limited additional information and committee assignments, with the Compensation Committee considered the most important here, composed of three board members.

Table A1.2 provides summary information about each director nominee. Each director is elected annually by a majority of votes cast.

Major stockholders are listed in Table A1.3. Not surprisingly, Cofounder and Chairman Bill Gates and chief executive officer (CEO)

Table A1.1 Proposal up for stockholder votes for 2013

Proposal number	Item	Votes required for approval	Abstentions	Uninstructed shares
1	Election of directors	Majority of shares cast	Not voted	Not voted
2	Performance criteria under the Executive Officer Incentive Plan	Majority of shares cast	Not voted	Not voted
3	Advisory vote on executive compensation (Say on Pay)	Majority of shares cast	Not voted	Not voted
4	Ratification of independent auditor	Majority of shares cast	Not voted	Discretionary vote

Table A1.2 Microsoft's directors subject to stockholder vote

Name	Age	Director since	Occupation	Independent	Other public boards	Committee memberships			
						AC	CC	GN	RPP
Steven A. Ballmer	57	2000	CEO, Microsoft		0				
Dina Dublon	60	2005	Former CFO and EVP, JP Morgan Chase & Co.	•	2	F	M		
William H. Gates III	57	1981	Chairman, Microsoft		1				
Maria M. Klawe	62	2009	President, Harvey Mudd College	•	1		M		M
Stephen J. Luczo	56	2012	CEO, Seagate Technology PLC	•	1	F	C		

(Continued)

Table A1.2 Microsoft's directors subject to stockholder vote (Continued)

Name	Age	Director since	Occupation	Independent	Other public boards	Committee memberships			
						AC	CC	GN	RPP
David F. Marquardt	64	1981	General Partner, August Capital	●	0			M	
Charles H. Noski	61	2003	Former Vice Chairman, Bank of America Corporation	●	2	C, F		M	
Helmut Panke	67	2003	Former Chairman of the Board of Management, BMW Bayerische Motoren Werke AG	●	3	F			C
John W. Thompson	64	2012	CEO, Virtual Instruments, Inc.	●	0			C	M

Note: C = Chair, F = Financial expert, M = Member, AC = Audit Committee, CC = Compensation Committee, GN = Governance and Nominating Committee, RPP = Regulatory and Public Policy Committee.

at the time, Steve Ballmer, led the list with 4.5 percent and 4.0 percent of outstanding shares, respectively, taking them high on the list of American's billionaires. None of the other executives/directors was even close to 1 percent; Venture Capitalist David Marquardt had the highest share

Table A1.3 Major stock ownership (Beneficial ownership table)

Name	Amount and nature of beneficial ownership of common shares as of 9/13/2013[1]	Percent of class
William H. Gates III	377,989,165[2]	4.52
Steven A. Ballmer	333,252,990	3.99
Dina Dublon	38,609[3]	*
Maria M. Klawe	22,336	*
Stephen J. Luczo	145,082[4]	*
David F. Marquardt	677,612[5]	*
Charles H. Noski	81,292[6]	*
Helmut Panke	41,840	*
John W. Thompson	5,151	*
Peter S. Klein	400	*
Amy E. Hood	71,113[7]	*
Kurt D. DelBene	13,921	*
Satya Nadella	113,666	*
B. Kevin Turner	218,520	*
Executive officers and directors as a group (19 persons)	714,362,908[8]	8.54
BlackRock, Inc. 40 East 52nd Street New York, NY 10022	468,957,475[9]	5.57

Note:
*Less than 1%
[1] Beneficial ownership represents sole voting and investment power.
[2] Excludes 424,816 shares held by Mr. Gates's spouse, as to which he disclaims beneficial ownership.
[3] Includes 16,738 shares representing deferred stock.
[4] Includes 11,582 shares representing deferred stock.
[5] Includes an aggregate of 3,975 shares held in trusts for three of Mr. Marquardt's children.
[6] Includes 69,112 shares representing deferred stock.
[7] Includes restricted stock units (RSUs) for 44,779 shares that will vest within 60 days of September 13, 2013 (RSU shares).
[8] Includes 97,432 shares representing deferred stock, 228,738 RSU shares, and 161,460 options to purchase Company stock exercisable within 60 days of September 13, 2013.
[9] All information about BlackRock, Inc. is based on a Schedule 13G filed with the SEC on February 11, 2013.

total of the also-rans at 677,612. Giant investment firm BlackRock was the big outsider, owning 5.6 percent.

The Proxy Statement provides reasonably detailed biographies for the board members running for election and three are presented as examples in Table A1.4, Gates, Ballmer, and Stephen Luczo, chairs of the compensation committee. Luczo was chairman (and formerly CEO) of Seagate Technology, a high-tech company. Compensation paid to the board members is summarized in Table A1.5, with total compensation ranging from $132,500 (prorated awards for two members only serving a partial year) to $280,000, generally about half in cash and half in stock awards.

Microsoft described their compensation objectives as follows (iii to iv):

Table A1.4 Selected board member biographies

Our director nominees

Steven A. Ballmer
Age: 57 years

Director since 2000

Mr. Ballmer has led several Microsoft divisions during the past 33 years, including operations, operating systems development, and sales and support. In July 1998, he was promoted as the president, a role that gave him day-to-day responsibility for running Microsoft. He was named Microsoft's chief executive officer in January 2000, assuming full management responsibility for the Company. In August 2013, Mr. Ballmer announced that he would be retiring as chief executive officer of Microsoft within the subsequent 12 months.

Public company directorships in the last five years:

- Microsoft Corporation

(Continued)

Qualifications:

Mr. Ballmer has deep knowledge of the Company's history, strategies, technologies, and culture. Mr. Ballmer has been the driving force behind the strategies and operational excellence that resulted in revenue tripling and operating income more than doubling since he became the chief executive officer in 2000. His leadership of diverse business units and functions before becoming chief executive officer gives Mr. Ballmer powerful insight into the product development, marketing, finance, and operations aspects of the Company. During his tenure, Mr. Ballmer has demonstrated the value of diversification of the company's business lines as he grew 13 additional businesses to more than $1 billion in revenues. He also led our expansion globally with international revenues growing from 32 percent to 47 percent of total annual revenues from 2000 to the present.

William H. Gates III
Age: 57 years

Director since 1981

Mr. Gates, a cofounder of Microsoft, has served as the chairman since our incorporation in 1981. Mr. Gates retired as an employee in July 2008, but continues to serve as an adviser on key development projects. Mr. Gates served as the chief software architect from January 2000 until June 2006, when he announced his two-year plan for transition out of a day-to-day full-time employee role. Mr. Gates served as our chief executive officer from 1981 until January 2000, when he resigned as chief executive officer and assumed the position of a chief software architect. As cochair of the Bill and Melinda Gates Foundation, Mr. Gates shapes and approves grant-making strategies, advocates for the foundation's issues, and helps set the overall direction of the organization.

Public company directorships in the last five years:

- Microsoft Corporation
- Berkshire Hathaway Inc.

Qualifications:

As a founder of Microsoft, Mr. Gates has unparalleled knowledge of the Company's history, strategies, technologies, and culture, and is considered a technology visionary. As chairman and chief executive officer of the Company from its incorporation in 1981 to 2000, he grew Microsoft from a fledgling business into the world's leading software company, in the process creating one of the world's most prolific sources of innovation and powerful brands. As the chief software architect from 2000 to 2006, and through 2008 when he retired as an employee of Microsoft, Mr. Gates set in motion many of the technological and strategic programs that animate the Company today. He continues to provide technical and strategic input on our continuing evolution as a devices and services company. His work overseeing the Bill and Melinda Gates Foundation provides global insights relevant to the Company's current and future business opportunities and a keen appreciation of stakeholder interests.

Stephen J. Luczo
Age: 56 years

Director since 2012

Mr. Luczo has been a director of Seagate Technology PLC (*Seagate*), since 2000, and has served as president and chief executive officer of Seagate since January 2009. He joined Seagate in 1993 as senior vice president of Corporate Development. In 1997, he was promoted as president and chief operating officer at Seagate Technology, Inc., and was promoted as the chief executive officer in 1998. He was appointed chairman of the board in 2002. He resigned his position as chief executive officer in 2004, but retained his position as chairman of the

(*Continued*)

board. From 2006 to 2009, he was a private investor. He rejoined Seagate as president and chief executive officer in January 2009. Prior to joining Seagate, Mr. Luczo was the senior managing director of the global technology group of an investment banking firm.

Public company directorships in the last five years:

- Microsoft Corporation
- Seagate Technology PLC.

Qualifications:

As president and chief executive officer of Seagate, a global leader in hard disk drives and storage solutions, Mr. Luczo brings substantial leadership experience in the field of hardware design and manufacturing, and cloud storage for consumers and enterprises. Mr. Luczo has direct responsibility for Seagate's strategy and operations, and his capabilities include executive leadership, global commerce and knowledge of competitive strategy, technology, and competition. With his early career based in investment banking, Mr. Luczo also brings to the Board significant mergers and acquisitions and financial experience related to business and financial issues facing large companies.

Table A1.5 Director compensation (Fiscal year 2013 director compensation)

Name	Fees earned or paid in cash[1] ($)	Stock awards ($)	Total ($)
Dina Dublon	122,500	150,000	272,500
William H. Gates III	100,000	150,000	250,000
Raymond V. Gilmartin[2]	57,500	75,000	132,500
Reed Hastings[3]	57,500	75,000	132,500
Maria M. Klawe	100,000	150,000	250,000
Stephen J. Luczo[4]	115,000	150,000	265,000
David F. Marquardt[5]	110,313	150,000	260,313
Charles H. Noski[6]	130,000	150,000	280,000
Helmut Panke	130,000	150,000	280,000
John W. Thompson[7]	115,000	150,000	265,000

Note:

[1] The value of fractional shares is excluded.

[2] Mr. Gilmartin's compensation was prorated for a partial year of service; he left the Board as of the 2012 annual meeting of shareholders.

[3] Mr. Hastings elected to defer both the cash and stock award components of his compensation. The combined cash and stock award value converted into 4,639 shares of our common stock. Delivery of the shares occurred 30 days after his separation from Board service. Mr. Hastings's compensation was prorated for a partial year of service; he left the Board as of the 2012 annual meeting of shareholders.

[4] Mr. Luczo elected to defer both the cash and stock award components of his compensation. The combined cash and stock award value converted into 8,943 shares of our common stock. Delivery of the shares will occur 30 days after the date of separation from Board service.

[5] Mr. Marquardt's compensation was prorated for his service as chair of the Finance Committee, which was dissolved effective July 24, 2012.

[6] Mr. Noski elected to defer both the cash and stock award components of his compensation in connection with his pay through January 2013. He revised his deferral election so that he would defer only the stock award component beginning with his May 2013 retainer. The combined cash and stock award value converted into 8,521 shares of our common stock. Delivery of the shares will occur 30 days after the date of separation from Board service.

[7] Mr. Thompson elected to defer the stock award component of his compensation. The stock award value converted into 5,061 shares of our common stock. Delivery of the shares will occur on the first anniversary after separation from Board service.

Pay for Performance

Our compensation program allows our Compensation Committee and Board to determine pay based on a comprehensive view of quantitative and qualitative factors designed to produce long-term business success. The correlation between our financial results and executive officer compensation awarded, as described in Part 4—"Named Executive Officer compensation—Compensation discussion and analysis," demonstrates the success of this approach.

Sound Program Design

We designed our executive officer compensation programs to attract, motivate, and retain the key executives who drive our success and industry leadership. Pay that reflects performance and alignment with the interests of long-term shareholders are key principles. We achieve our objectives through compensation that:

- Provides a competitive total pay opportunity,
- Consists primarily of stock-based compensation,
- Links a significant portion of total compensation to performance we believe will create long-term shareholder value,

- Differentiates rewards based on the executive officer's contributions to business performance,
- Enhances retention by subjecting much of total compensation to multiyear vesting, and
- Does not encourage unnecessary and excessive risk taking.

Best Practices in Executive Compensation

Our compensation programs for our Named Executive Officers incentivize superior individual and business performance and do not reward inappropriate risk taking. Some of our leading practices include:

- An executive compensation recovery policy,
- An executive stock ownership policy,
- A policy prohibiting pledging and hedging ownership of Microsoft stock,
- No special perquisites or benefits,
- No employment contracts or change in control protections, and
- No supplemental executive or similar retirement programs.

The remaining tables deal specifically with executive compensation (Part 4 of the Proxy Statement) in considerable detail. Table A1.6 describes the six major responsibilities of the Compensation Committee. The Committee uses the consulting group Semler Brossy. According to the write-up, *Semler Brossy is directly accountable to the Committee* and maintains its independence based on Microsoft's *Compensation Consultant Independence Standards* (which are stated in Table A1.6). Table A1.7 describes the setting of the executive pay process in three steps, while Table A1.8 compares Microsoft to two sets of *peer groups*: (1) technology competitors and (2) other members of the DOW. Table A1.7 suggested that fiscal year 2013 was a mixed year, with increases in revenues and unearned revenues, but decreases in both operating income and diluted earnings per share. The peer group analysis showed that Microsoft paid out a higher percentage of equity-based pay relative to competitors, but CEO Steve Ballmer received only $2.1 million in total compensation compared to an average $16 million for peer CEOs.

Table A1.6 Compensation committee responsibilities

Compensation Committee

The primary responsibilities of the Compensation Committee are to:

- assist our Board of Directors in establishing the annual goals and objectives of the chief executive officer,
- recommend to the independent members of our Board the compensation of the chief executive officer,
- oversee an evaluation of the performance of the Company's other executive officers and approve their compensation,
- oversee and advise our Board on the adoption of policies that govern executive officer compensation programs and other compensation-related polices,
- assist the Board in overseeing plans for executive officer development and succession, and
- oversee administration of our equity-based compensation and other benefit plans.

Our senior executives for human resources and compensation and benefits support the Compensation Committee in its work. The Committee may delegate to senior management the authority to make equity compensation grants to employees who are not executive officers. The Compensation Committee periodically reviews the compensation paid to nonemployee directors, and makes recommendations to our Board of Directors for any adjustments.

The Compensation Committee Charter describes the specific responsibilities and functions of the Compensation Committee. See Part 4—"Named Executive Officer compensation—Compensation discussion and analysis" for more information about the Committee's work.

Compensation Consultant

The Committee retains Semler Brossy Consulting Group, LLC, to advise the Committee on marketplace trends in executive compensation, management proposals for compensation programs, and executive officer compensation decisions. Semler Brossy also evaluates compensation for the next levels of senior management and equity

(Continued)

compensation programs generally. It also consults with the Committee about its recommendations to the Board of Directors on chief executive officer and director compensation.

Consultant Independence

Semler Brossy is directly accountable to the Committee. To maintain the independence of the firm's advice, Semler Brossy does not provide any services for Microsoft other than those described above. The Committee has adopted Compensation Consultant Independence Standards, which can be viewed at *www.microsoft.com/investor/comp-consultant*. This policy requires that the Committee annually assess the independence of its compensation consultant. A consultant satisfying the following requirements will be considered independent. The consultant (including each individual employee of the consultant providing services):

- is retained and terminated by, has its compensation fixed by, and reports solely to the Committee,
- is independent of the Company,
- will not perform any work for Company management except at the request of the Committee chair and in the capacity of the Committee's agent, and
- does not provide any unrelated services or products to the Company, its affiliates, or management, except for surveys purchased from the consultant firm.

In performing the annual assessment of the consultant's independence, the Committee considers the nature and amount of work performed for the Committee during the year, the nature of any unrelated services performed for the Company, and the amount of fees paid for those services in relation to the firm's total revenues. The consultant annually prepares for the Committee an independence letter providing appropriate assurances and confirmation of the consultant's independent status pursuant to the policy. The Committee believes that Semler Brossy has been independent during its service for the Committee.

Table A1.7 Executive compensation process

Section 1—Performance and pay

Fiscal year 2013 corporate performance

Company-wide performance

In fiscal year 2013, we made significant strides in our evolution to a devices and services company. At the same time, our results demonstrated that this is a long-term process and reflected a mixed environment for many of our key products and services. Areas of strength included our offerings for the enterprise and cloud services for consumers and businesses. Challenges included a declining personal computer (PC) market and slower than anticipated sales of Surface runtime (RT) devices, which resulted in our decision to reduce prices to accelerate sales and a $900 million inventory charge.

Key fiscal year 2013 financial results we reported were:

- $77.31 billion in revenue as adjusted,* an increase of 4 percent (generally accepted accounting principles [GAAP] revenue of $77.85 billion)
- $26.96 billion in operating income as adjusted,* a decrease of 5 percent (GAAP operating income of $26.76 billion)
- $2.62 diluted earnings per share as adjusted,* a decrease of 6 percent (GAAP diluted earnings per share of $2.58)
- $22.4 billion in unearned revenue as of fiscal year end, a record amount
- $12.3 billion returned to shareholders through dividends and stock buybacks

*Revenue adjusted for revenue deferrals from sales of Windows 7 with an option to upgrade to Windows 8 Pro at a discounted price (the *Windows Upgrade Offer*). Operating income and EPS adjusted for Windows Upgrade Offer deferral, goodwill impairment and European Commission fine. Please see Annex A to this Proxy Statement for a reconciliation of non-GAAP and GAAP financial measures presented.

(Continued)

Table A1.7 Executive compensation process (Continued)

Section 2—Compensation setting process and decisions for fiscal year 2013

Executive compensation program

In fiscal year 2013, we continued to provide executive officer compensation via a straightforward structure consisting of base salary and incentive awards under our Executive Officer Incentive Plan (*Incentive Plan*). Our executive compensation program incentivizes performance and does not reward inappropriate risk taking as further described below in Section 3—*Other compensation policies and information*—and in Part 6—"Proposals to be voted on at the meeting—Advisory vote on executive compensation."

As in previous years, Mr. Ballmer's incentive compensation opportunity for fiscal year 2013 was limited to a cash award of up to 200 percent of his fiscal year 2013 base salary, consistent with his long-standing request that we not award him equity compensation. The fiscal year 2013 Incentive Plan awards for other executive officers were paid as

- a cash award payable in September 2013, and
- a stock award granted in September 2012 that vests in four equal installments, with the first installment vesting in September 2013 and subsequent installments vesting on August 31 in each of the following three years.

The stock award is a restricted stock unit that is settled in Microsoft common stock. For stock awards granted at the beginning of the fiscal year, the number of shares subject to each stock award is determined by dividing the award value by the closing price of Microsoft common stock on the last business day in August of that fiscal year.

As in prior years, the fiscal year 2013 compensation decisions for our executive officers were made in three steps.

(Continued)

Roles of Board, Compensation Committee, and CEO	Steps	When
• CEO compensation decisions are made by the independent members of the Board, based on recommendation of the Compensation Committee	Design Program—Program for year is approved (including mix of annual and multiyear pay, fixed and incentive compensation, and any base salary adjustment)	Beginning of fiscal year
• Other named executive officer (NEO) compensation decisions are made by the Compensation Committee, based on recommendations of the CEO	Establish Range of Compensation Opportunities—Incentive compensation opportunities are set (minimum, target, and maximum incentive awards)	Beginning of fiscal year
• The Compensation Committee is advised by an independent compensation consultant	Review Performance—Performance is reviewed, which leads to decisions about actual Incentive Plan award amounts	Following end of fiscal year

Table A1.8 Peer group analysis

In mid-2012, when we were preparing our fiscal year 2013 compensation design and establishing target compensation opportunities, the two peer groups consisted of these companies.

Technology peer group		Dow 30 peer group		
Accenture	IBM*	3M	DuPont	Pfizer
Adobe Systems	Intel*	Alcoa	Exxon Mobil	Procter &
Amazon	Oracle	American	General Electric	Gamble
Apple	SAP	Express	Home Depot	Travelers
BlackBerry	Symantec	AT&T	JP Morgan	Companies
Cisco Systems*	Yahoo	Bank of	Chase	United Tech-
Dell Computer		America	Johnson &	nologies
Google		Boeing	Johnson	Verizon
Hewlett-Packard*		Caterpillar	Kraft Foods	Wal-Mart
		Chevron	(now	Walt Disney
		Coca-Cola	Mondelez)	
			McDonald's	
			Merck	

[* competitors]

(Continued)

Pay mix versus peers

Peer group   Microsoft

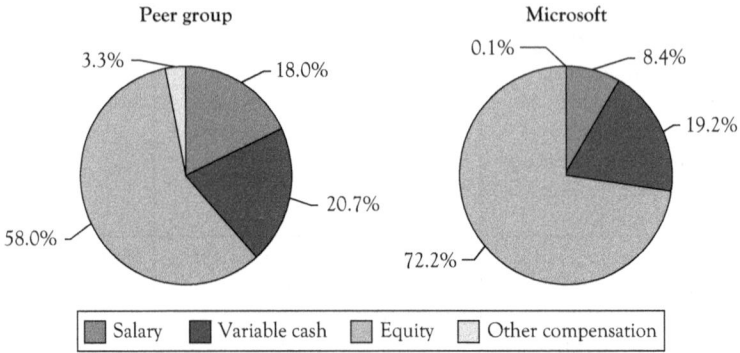

Salary   Variable cash   Equity   Other compensation

Peer group companies. Variable cash consists of discretionary bonuses, target annual nonequity incentive plan awards, and target multiyear nonequity incentive plan awards. Equity consists of stock options, stock awards, annual incentive plan equity awards, and multiyear incentive plan equity awards.

CEO pay comparison

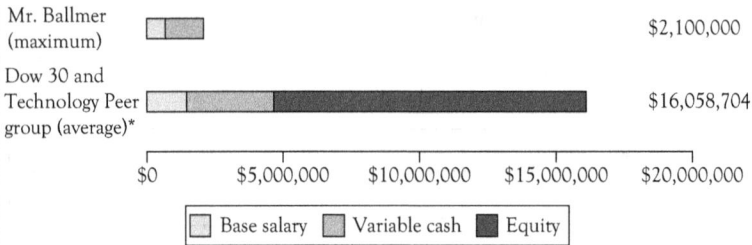

Base salary   Variable cash   Equity

* Excludes chief executive officers with atypical pay structures such as founders. Figures are based on publicly available information as of August 2013. For peers, values are target compensation.

Table A1.9 describes other compensation, usually relatively small amounts, but potentially important in terms of items that are generally not available to other employees and could cause various accounting issues. Microsoft benefits include those available to all employees such as a 401(k) plan, health and life insurance coverage, and deferred compensation plans.

The company was unusual because it has few termination benefits, although stock vesting continues after employees retire (at age 65 years or 55 years with 15 years of service). Claw back provisions exist and are explained under *Executive Compensation Recovery Policy*. Table A1.10 reviews Microsoft's annual compensation risk assessment (for potential *materially adverse effects*). Presumably, compensation does not incentivize excessive risk taking nor short-term performance.

Table A1.9 Other compensation

Other compensation policies and information

Executive benefits and perquisites

Our Named Executive Officers are eligible for the same benefits available to our other U.S.-based full-time employees, including our Section 401(k) plan, employee stock purchase plan, health care plan, life insurance plans, and other welfare benefit programs. In addition to the standard benefits offered to all employees, we maintain a nonqualified deferred compensation plan for our executives and senior managers. The deferred compensation plan is unfunded, and participation is voluntary. The deferred compensation plan allows our Named Executive Officers to defer their base salary, the cash portion of their Incentive Plan awards, and certain on-hire bonuses. We do not contribute to the nonqualified deferred compensation plan.

Post-employment compensation

Our Named Executive Officers do not have employment contracts, and they are not entitled to any payments or benefits following a change in control of Microsoft. They may be eligible for the following payments or benefits upon termination of their employment:

- All employees who retire from Microsoft in the United States after (a) age 65 years or (b) age 55 years with 15 years of service are eligible for the continuation of vesting of

(*Continued*)

Table A1.9 Other compensation (Continued)

stock awards granted at hire or at performance review, if they were granted more than one year before retirement.

- Generally, all employees whose employment with Microsoft terminates due to death or total and permanent disability will fully vest in their outstanding stock awards.
- In September 2013, the Compensation Committee implemented a Senior Executive Severance Benefit Plan that is described in *Fiscal year 2014 compensation changes* in Section 2 above.
- Pursuant to Mr. Turner's employment offer letter, 160,000 shares of his on-hire stock award will vest upon his retirement from Microsoft at age 60 years or older.
- In connection with Mr. Klein's resignation from his position as chief financial officer, Mr. Klein agreed to continue in that position until his successor was appointed and he remained an employee of the Company through June 30, 2013. The Company will pay Mr. Klein $1,000,000 on January 15, 2014, and $1,000,000 on June 30, 2014, as compensation for his services during fiscal year 2013 and performance of his obligations under his resignation agreement.

Executive compensation recovery policy

Accountability is a fundamental value of Microsoft. To reinforce this value through our executive compensation program, our executive officers and certain other senior executives are subject to an executive compensation recovery policy. Under this policy, the Committee may seek to recover payments of incentive compensation if the performance results leading to a payment are later subject to a downward adjustment or restatement of financial or nonfinancial performance. The Committee may use its judgment in determining the amount to be recovered where the incentive compensation was awarded on a discretionary basis, as with awards under the Incentive Plan. The Committee may recover incentive compensation whether or not the executive's actions

> involve misconduct. When an executive has engaged in intentional misconduct that contributed to the payment, the Committee may take other remedial action, including seeking to recover the entire payment.

Table A1.10 Compensation risks

Compensation risk assessment

We performed an annual assessment for the Compensation and Audit Committees of our Board of Directors to determine whether the risks arising from any of our fiscal year 2013 compensation policies or practices are reasonably likely to have a material adverse effect on the Company. Our assessment reviewed material elements of executive and non-executive employee compensation. We concluded that these policies and practices do not create risk that is reasonably likely to have a material adverse effect on the Company.

In addition, the structure of our compensation program for executive officers does not incentivize unnecessary or excessive risk taking. The base salary component of compensation does not encourage risk-taking because it is a fixed amount. The Incentive Plan awards have the following risk-limiting characteristics:

- Awards to each executive officer are limited to the lesser of a fixed maximum specified in the Incentive Plan, and a fixed percentage of an incentive pool. Cash awards under the Incentive Plan are limited to 300 percent of a target cash award (200 percent of base salary for Mr. Ballmer).
- Cash awards are based on a review of a variety performance factors, thus diversifying the risk associated with any single aspect of performance, while amounts received under stock awards do not vary directly based on an individual executive officer's performance.
- Awards are not made in the form of stock options, which may provide an asymmetrical incentive to take unnecessary or excessive risks to increase Company stock price.

(Continued)

Table A1.10 Compensation risks (Continued)

- Awards are not tied to formulas that could focus executives on specific short-term outcomes.
- Members of the Compensation Committee, or in the case of Mr. Ballmer, the independent members of our Board of Directors, approve the final Incentive Plan cash awards in their discretion, after reviewing executive and corporate performance.
- Awards are subject to our Executive Compensation Recovery Policy, described in Part 4 "Named Executive Officer compensation—Other compensation policies and information—Executive compensation recovery policy."
- For executive officers other than Mr. Ballmer, the majority of the award value is delivered in the form of shares of common stock with a multiyear vesting schedule, which aligns the interests of our executive officers to long-term shareholder interests. For Mr. Ballmer, this alignment exists by virtue of his being one of Microsoft's largest shareholders.
- Executive officers are subject to our executive stock ownership requirements described in Part 4—"Named Executive Officer compensation—Other compensation policies and information—Stock ownership policy."

Table A1.11 has the compensation tables for the six *Named Executive Officers*. Perhaps, the most important disclosure is the summary compensation table (three years) for the six top executives, presented in Table A1.11a, which explains both the magnitudes and types of pay for the senior people. Steve Ballmer, the outgoing CEO (he was replaced by Satya Nadella in February of 2014—his 2013 pay was $7.7 million), received a relatively small salary and cash bonus and no stock awards. This probably had more to do with the extraordinary options and other awards he received earlier in his career at Microsoft (making him one of the world's richest men at over $20 billion) than the current performance of Microsoft. Kevin Turner, chief operating officer, was Microsoft's higher-paid executive at $10.4 million with almost $7.5 million coming from about 260,000 restricted stock shares. Amy Hood was named the chief financial officer (CFO) in May 2013; thus, her $7.5 million in total compensation represents only a partial year's pay. About half of that represented the 100,000 plus restricted shares (worth $3.3 million) she received upon her promotion as CFO. Microsoft had in earlier years paid out extensive stock options as did most tech companies, but changed the policy to mainly restricted stock in 2004.

Table A1.11 Fiscal year 2013 compensation tables: (a) summary compensation table; (b) all other compensation; (c) grants of plan-based awards for fiscal year ended June 30, 2013; (d) outstanding equity awards as of June 30, 2013; (e) vesting dates and number of shares; (f) option exercises and stock awards vested for fiscal year ended June 30, 2013; and (g) nonqualified deferred compensation

The following table contains information about compensation awarded to our Named Executive Officers for the fiscal years ended June 30, 2013, June 30, 2012, and June 30, 2011. None of our Named Executive Officers received stock options during those fiscal years.

(a)

Name and principal position	Year	Salary ($)	Bonus[1] ($)	Stock awards[2] ($)	All other compensation[3] ($)	Total ($)
Steven A. Ballmer, chief executive officer and director	2013	697,500	550,000	N/A	13,718	1,261,218
	2012	685,000	620,000	N/A	13,128	1,318,128
	2011	682,500	682,500	N/A	11,915	1,376,915
Amy E. Hood, chief financial officer	2013	365,954	457,443	6,626,019[3]	11,153	7,460,569

(*Continued*)

Table A1.11 (Continued)

Name and principal position	Year	Salary ($)	Bonus[1] ($)	Stock awards[2] ($)	All other compe-nsation[3] ($)	Total ($)
Peter S. Klein, former chief financial officer	2013	598,333	N/A	3,542,323	11,820	4,152,476
	2012	580,000	950,000	3,567,806	11,030	5,108,836
	2011	525,000	720,000	2,266,321	10,366	3,521,687
Kurt D. DelBene, president, Microsoft Office Division	2013	669,167	1,505,625	5,406,699	10,954	7,592,445
	2012	638,333	1,812,500	5,445,594	10,298	7,906,725
	2011	603,333	1,450,000	4,154,922	10,994	6,219,249
Satya Nadella, president, Server and Tools	2013	669,167	1,580,906	5,406,699	12,180	7,668,952
B. Kevin Turner, chief operating officer	2013	777,500	2,138,125	7,457,504	10,484	10,383,613
	2012	762,500	2,400,000	7,511,150	10,021	10,683,671
	2011	732,500	1,925,000	6,610,104	9,537	9,277,141

Note:

[1] This column reports Incentive Plan awards for the fiscal year that were paid in cash in September following the fiscal year end.

[2] This column reports the Incentive Plan stock awards for the fiscal year, and any other stock awards granted outside the Incentive Plan during fiscal year 2013. All amounts in this column are calculated using the grant date fair value under Accounting Standards Codification Topic 718 based on the market price as of the date of grant of common stock awarded, reduced by the present value of estimated future dividends because the awards are not entitled to receive dividends prior to vesting.

[3] Ms. Hood's fiscal year 2013 amount includes an award of 103,413 shares (with a grant date fair value of $3,319,557) she received in connection with her promotion as chief financial officer. Her stock award amount also includes 21,617 shares (with a grant date fair value of $639,215) awarded during fiscal year 2013 for her fiscal year 2012 performance in her prior role.

(b)

Name	Year	Relocation expense ($)	Tax gross up ($)	401(k) Company match ($)	Income received under broad-based benefits program* ($)	Total ($)
Steven A. Ballmer	2013	0	0	7,650	6,068	13,718
	2012	0	0	7,500	5,628	13,128
	2011	0	0	7,350	4,565	11,915
Amy E. Hood	2013	0	0	8,614	2,539	11,153
Peter S. Klein	2013	0	0	7,650	4,170	11,820
	2012	0	0	7,500	3,530	11,030
	2011	0	0	7,350	3,016	10,366
Kurt D. DelBene	2013	0	0	7,763	3,191	10,954
	2012	0	0	7,430	2,868	10,298
	2011	0	0	8,545	2,449	10,994
Satya Nadella	2013	0	0	7,650	4,530	12,180
B. Kevin Turner	2013	0	0	7,650	2,834	10,484
	2012	0	0	7,500	2,521	10,021
	2011	0	0	7,350	2,187	9,537

* These amounts include (i) imputed income from life and disability insurance, and (ii) athletic club membership and payments in lieu of athletic club membership. These benefits are available to substantially all our U.S.-based employees.

(c)

Name	Grant date	Approval date	Stock awards (#)	Grant date fair value of stock awards,[1] ($)
Steven A. Ballmer	N/A	N/A	N/A	N/A
Amy E. Hood	8/31/2012	8/30/2012	36,422[2]	1,045,917
	8/31/2012	8/30/2012	21,617[3]	639,215
	5/15/2013	5/15/2013	103,413[4]	3,319,557

(*Continued*)

Name	Grant date	Approval date	Stock awards (#)	Grant date fair value of stock awards,[1] ($)
	5/15/2013	5/15/2013	82,731[5]	2,667,247
Peter S. Klein	9/10/2012	9/10/2012	123,297	3,542,323
Kurt D. DelBene	9/10/2012	9/10/2012	188,190	5,406,699
Satya Nadella	9/10/2012	9/10/2012	188,190	5,406,699
B. Kevin Turner	9/10/2012	9/10/2012	259,572	7,457,504

Note:

[1] All amounts in this column are calculated using the grant date fair value under Accounting Standards Codification Topic 718 based on the market price as of the date of grant of common stock awarded, reduced by the present value of estimated future dividends because the awards are not entitled to receive dividends prior to vesting.

[2] Represents stock awards granted to Ms. Hood before her promotion as chief financial officer, which were rescinded and reissued with an award having terms consistent with stock awards under the Incentive Plan for fiscal year 2013 in connection with the promotion.

[3] Represents an award Ms. Hood received during fiscal year 2013 for her fiscal year 2012 performance in her prior role.

[4] Represents an award Ms. Hood received in connection with her promotion to Chief Financial Officer.

[5] Represents the reissued award Ms. Hood received under the Incentive Plan as compensation in her expanded role as chief financial officer.

(d)

	Stock awards	
Name	Number of shares or units of stock that have not vested[1] ($)	Market value of shares or units of stock that have not vested[2] ($)
Steven A. Ballmer	N/A	N/A
Amy E. Hood	290,534	10,036,497
Peter S. Klein	N/A	N/A
Kurt D. DelBene	500,999	17,307,010
Satya Nadella	454,062	15,685,572
B. Kevin Turner	881,454	30,449,828

[1] The following table shows the dates on which the awards in the outstanding equity awards table vest and the corresponding number of shares, subject to continued employment through the vest date.

[2] The market value is the number of shares shown in the table multiplied by $34.545, the closing market price of Microsoft common stock on June 28, 2013.

(e)

Vesting date	Amy Hood	Kurt D. DelBene	Satya Nadella	B. Kevin Turner
	Number of shares vesting			

Vesting date	Amy Hood	Kurt D. DelBene	Satya Nadella	B. Kevin Turner
8/29/2013	0	3,665	5,497	0
8/31/2013	20,682	178,786	169,186	298,662
9/28/2013	37,237	0	0	0
10/24/2013	3,518	0	0	0
10/26/2013	4,024	0	0	0
5/15/2014	41,365	0	0	0
8/31/2014	20,683	165,643	140,588	215,134
9/28/2014	31,565	0	0	0
10/26/2014	4,025	0	0	0
5/15/2015	31,024	0	0	0
8/31/2015	20,683	105,857	91,743	142,765
9/28/2015	20,299	0	0	0
5/15/2016	31,024	0	0	0
8/31/2016	20,683	47,048	47,048	64,893
9/28/2016	3,722	0	0	0
Retirement at age 60 years or older (year 2025)	0	0	0	160,000
Total	290,534	500,999	454,062	881,454

(f)

Name	Option awards		Stock awards	
	Number of shares acquired on exercise (#)	Value realized on exercise[1] ($)	Number of shares acquired on vesting (#)	Value realized on vesting[2] (#)
Steven A. Ballmer	N/A	N/A	N/A	N/A
Amy E. Hood	11,111	36,250	49,624	1,467,236

(Continued)

| | Option awards | | Stock awards | |
| | Number of shares acquired on exercise (#) | Value realized on exercise[1] ($) | Number of shares acquired on vesting (#) | Value realized on vesting[2] (#) |
Name				
Peter S. Klein	N/A	N/A	96,962	2,972,607
Kurt D. DelBene	N/A	N/A	145,193	4,463,667
Satya Nadella	N/A	N/A	163,137	4,957,870
B. Kevin Turner	N/A	N/A	272,389	8,338,652

[1] The value realized on exercise is calculated as the difference between the market price of the shares underlying the options at exercise and the applicable exercise price of those options.
[2] The value realized on vesting is calculated by multiplying the number of shares shown in the table by the market value of the shares on the vesting date.

The following table provides information about Named Executive Officers' contributions, earnings, and balances under our nonqualified deferred compensation plan in fiscal year 2013. Microsoft does not

(g)

Name	Executive contributions in fiscal year 2013[1] ($)	Aggregate earnings in fiscal year 2013[2] ($)	Aggregate balance at June 30, 2013 ($)
Steven A. Ballmer	N/A	N/A	N/A
Amy E. Hood	N/A	N/A	N/A
Peter S. Klein	N/A	N/A	N/A
Kurt D. Del-Bene	334,583	1,327,878	7,880,173
Satya Nadella	N/A	15,525	132,670
B. Kevin Turner	N/A	N/A	N/A

[1] The amount in this column includes $334,583 deferred from fiscal year 2013 salary, which is reported in the Salary Column of the Summary Compensation Table.
[2] The amount in this column is not included in the Summary Compensation Table because plan earnings were not preferential or above-market.

contribute to the deferred compensation plan, and in fiscal year 2013, there were no withdrawals by or distributions to Named Executive Officers.

Microsoft's deferred compensation plan is unfunded and unsecured. It allows participants to defer a specified percentage of their base salary (upto 50 percent), eligible incentive cash payments (upto 100 percent), or both. Participation in the deferred compensation plan is limited to senior management, including our Named Executive Officers. Microsoft does not contribute to the deferred compensation plan or guarantee any returns on participant contributions.

At the time an employee elects to participate in the deferred compensation plan, the employee must specify the percentage of base salary, cash incentive award to be deferred, or both, as well as the timing of distributions. If employment terminates before retirement (defined as at least of age 55 years with 10 years of service, or age 65 years), distribution is made in the form of a lump sum following termination. At retirement, benefits are paid according to the distribution election made by the participant at the time of the deferral election. No withdrawals are permitted during employment or prior to the previously elected distribution date, other than *hardship withdrawals* as permitted by applicable law. Amounts deferred under the deferred compensation plan are credited with hypothetical investment earnings based on participant investment elections made from among investment options available under the plan.

Table A1.11b summarized other compensation, mainly 401(k) contributions and insurance. Table A1.11c described stock awards, mainly based on grants from 2012. The value of these ranged from zero for Steve Ballmer to $7.5 million for Kevin Turner. The market value of outstanding stock awards, Table A1.11d, ranged up to $30.5 million for Turner, while vesting dates were stated in Table A1.11e up through 2016. Table A1.11f shows the split between options and restricted stock, with almost all awards restricted stock. Nonqualified deferred compensation is presented in Table A1.11g, with only Kurt DelBene and Satya Nadella participating.

APPENDIX 2

Microsoft 10-K Stock Compensation Disclosures, 2013

In addition to the executive compensation disclosures in the Proxy Statement, Microsoft had stock compensation and savings plans available for all employees, presented as Note 20 in the 2013 10-k. Stock-related compensation included restricted stock associated with *leadership stock awards* (LSAs) and the *executive incentive plan* (EIP), stock options mainly related to acquisitions, an employee stock purchase plan, and a 401(k) plan. Common to corporations, even large corporations, started after 1980, Microsoft has no defined benefit pension plan and little or nothing in the way of other post-employment benefits.

The restricted stock plans are performance based, usually vesting over five years. The LSAs are based on *certain performance metrics* that are not specifically stated in the Note. The EIP awards are calculated as a percentage of consolidated operating income. The pool for 2013 was 0.35 percent of operating income ($26,776 million), which would be $93.7 million (0.35 percent × $26,776 million). During 2013, 104 million shares were granted, 90 million shares vested (fair value of $2.8 billion), and 273 million remained non-vested.

Microsoft switched from options to restricted stock in 2004. However, stock options were still used *primarily in conjunction with business acquisitions*. During 2013, 2 million options were granted, 19 million exercised, 1 million canceled, leaving a year-end balance of 4 million. Employees were allowed to purchase Microsoft shares at quarterly intervals at 90 percent of fair value (last trading day of each quarter) up to 15 percent of the gross compensation. During 2013, some 20 million shares were purchased. The 401(k) plan allowed employees to contribute up to 6 percent of the salary and receive a matching of 3 percent (i.e., Microsoft would contribute $0.50 for each employee dollar contributed). Beyond that, the employees could contribute a total 75 percent of salary but without matching. Microsoft's 2013 contributions totaled $393 million.

Note 20—Employee Stock and Savings Plans

We grant stock-based compensation to directors and employees. At June 30, 2013, an aggregate of 425 million shares were authorized for future grant under our stock plans, covering stock options, stock awards (SAs), and LSAs. Awards that expire or are canceled without delivery of shares generally become available for issuance under the plans. We issue new shares of Microsoft common stock to satisfy exercises and vesting of awards granted under all of our stock plans.

Stock-based compensation expense and related income tax benefits were as follows:

	In million $, year ended June 30,		
	2013	2012	2011
Stock-based compensation expense	2,406	2,244	2,166
Income tax benefits related to stock-based compensation	842	785	758

Stock Plans (Excluding Stock Options)

Stock Awards

SAs are grants that entitle the holder to shares of Microsoft common stock as the award vests. SAs generally vest over a five-year period.

Leadership Stock Awards

LSAs are a form of SAs in which the number of shares ultimately received depends on our business performance against specified performance metrics. LSAs replaced shared performance stock awards (SPSA) in fiscal year

2013. Shares previously issued under the SPSA program will continue to vest ratably under their original term, generally with a three-year remaining service period.

A base number of LSAs are granted in each fiscal year, which represents the performance period for the awards. Following the end of the performance period, the number of shares can be increased by 25 percent if certain performance metrics are met. One quarter of the awarded shares will vest one year after the grant date. The remaining shares will vest semi-annually during the following three years.

Executive Incentive Plan

Under the EIP, the Compensation Committee awards performance-based compensation comprising both cash and SAs to executive officers and certain senior executives. For executive officers, their awards are based on an aggregate incentive pool equal to a percentage of consolidated operating income. For fiscal years 2013, 2012, and 2011, the pool was 0.35 percent, 0.3 percent, and 0.25 percent of operating income, respectively. The SAs vest ratably in August of each of the four years following the grant date. The final cash awards will be determined after each performance period based on individual and business performance.

Activity For All Stock Plans

The fair value of each award was estimated on the date of grant using the following assumptions:

| | Year ended June 30, | | |
	2013	2012	2011 ($)
Dividends per share (quarterly amounts)	$0.20–0.23	$0.16–0.20	$0.13–0.16
Interest rate range	0.6%–1.1%	0.7%–1.7%	1.1%–2.4%

During fiscal year 2013, the following activity occurred under our stock plans:

	Shares (in millions)	Weighted average grant-date fair value ($)
SAs		
Nonvested balance, beginning of year	281	23.91
Granted	104	28.37
Vested	90	24.49
Forfeited	22	25.10
Nonvested balance, end of year	273	25.50

As of June 30, 2013, there was approximately $5.0 billion of total unrecognized compensation costs related to SAs. These costs are expected to be recognized over a weighted average period of three years.

During fiscal years 2012 and 2011, the following activity occurred under our stock plans:

(In millions, except fair values)	2012	2011
SAs		
Awards granted	110	132
Weighted average grant-date fair value	$24.60	$22.22

Total vest-date fair values of SAs vested were $2.8 billion, $2.4 billion, and $1.8 billion, for fiscal years 2013, 2012, and 2011, respectively.

Stock Options

Currently, we grant stock options primarily in conjunction with business acquisitions. We granted two million, six million, and zero stock options in conjunction with business acquisitions during fiscal years 2013, 2012, and 2011, respectively.

Employee stock options activity during 2013 was as follows:

	Shares (in millions)	Weighted average exercise price ($)	Weighted average remaining contractual term (Years)	Aggregate intrinsic value (in million $)
Balance, July 1, 2012	22	18.69		
Granted	2	2.08		
Exercised	19	19.26		
Canceled	1	14.71		
Balance, June 30, 2013	4	6.88	6.74	98
Exercisable, June 30, 2013	2	8.47	5.79	50

As of June 30, 2013, approximately four million options that were granted in conjunction with business acquisitions were outstanding. These options have an exercise price range of $0.01 to $29.24 and a weighted average exercise price of $7.33.

During the periods reported, the following stock option exercise activity occurred:

(In millions)	2013 ($)	2012 ($)	2011 ($)
Total intrinsic value of stock options exercised	197	456	222
Cash received from stock option exercises	382	1,410	1,954
Tax benefit realized from stock option exercises	69	160	77

Employee Stock Purchase Plan

We have an employee stock purchase plan (the *Plan*) for all eligible employees. Shares of our common stock may be purchased by employees at three-month intervals at 90 percent of the fair market value on the last trading day of each three-month period. Employees may purchase shares having a value not exceeding 15 percent of their gross compensation during an offering period. Employees purchased the following shares during the periods presented:

(Shares in millions)	Year ended June 30,		
	2013	2012	2011
Shares purchased	20	20	20
Average price per share	$26.81	$25.03	$22.98

At June 30, 2013, 191 million shares of our common stock were reserved for future issuance through the Plan.

Savings Plan

We have a savings plan in the United States that qualifies under Section 401(k) of the Internal Revenue Code, and a number of savings plans in international locations. Participating U.S. employees may contribute up to 75 percent of their salary, but not more than statutory limits. We contribute 50 cents for each dollar a participant contributes in this plan, with a maximum contribution of 3 percent of a participant's earnings. Matching contributions for all plans were $393 million, $373 million, and $282 million in fiscal years 2013, 2012, and 2011, respectively, and were expensed as contributed. Matching contributions are invested proportionate to each participant's voluntary contributions in the investment options provided under the plan. Investment options in the U.S. plan include Microsoft common stock, but neither participant nor our matching contributions are required to be invested in Microsoft common stock.

APPENDIX 3

Pfizer 10-k Disclosures, 2012

Pfizer, Inc., is a large biopharmaceutical manufacturer and a member of the Dow Jones Industrial Average (DOW). With a market capitalization about $200 billion, it is one of America's largest corporations. Pfizer's financial disclosures for fiscal year 2012 will be used (based on the 2012 10-K) to present the extensive disclosures required by public corporations for both compensation and retirement reporting. Note 13 in the 2012 10-k describes share-based payments: "Our compensation programs can include share-based payments, in the form of stock options, Restricted Stock Units (RSUs), Portfolio Performance Shares (PPSs), Performance Share Awards (PSAs) and Total Shareholder Return Units (TSRUs)." Table A3.1 shows the share-based expenses of $332 million net of tax (1.6 percent of 2012 net income). The major components were RSUs ($235 million or 48.9 percent of share-based expenses before tax) and stock options ($157 million or 32.6 percent).

Table A3.1 Impact of share-based expenses on net income, Pfizer, 2012

(Millions of dollars)	Year ended December 31,		
	2012	2011	2010
RSUs	235	228	211
Stock options	157	166	150
TSRUs	35	17	28
PSAs	35	3	14
PPSs	14	—	—
Directors' compensation and other	5	5	2
Share-based payment expense	481	419	405
Tax benefit for share-based compensation expense	149	139	129
Share-based payment expense, net of tax	332	280	276

There were three stock-based plans available to *selected employees*, with the calculations shown in Table A3.2: (a) RSUs nonvested, (b) stock options outstanding at the end of 2012, and (c) nonvested PPSs at Pfizer, fiscal year-end, 2012. The PPSs are basically performance-based restricted stock. There were 37.9 million RSUs nonvested, 383.0 million options outstanding, and 3.7 million PPSs (share-based expense of $14 million). In addition were two share-based plans available only to top management, both performance based. The TSRUs are long term and vest only after five to seven years, while the PPSs vest within three years (each with share-based expenses of $35 million).

Table A3.2 Calculation of (a) RSUs nonvested, (b) stock options outstanding at the end of 2012, and (c) nonvested PPSs at Pfizer, fiscal year-end, 2012

(a) The table summarizes all RSU activity during 2012

	Shares (thousands)	Weighted-average grant-date fair value per share ($)
Nonvested, December 31, 2011	41,940	17.08
Granted	13,232	21.05
Vested	15,464	15.09
Reinvested dividend equivalents	1,585	22.95
Forfeited	3,433	19.17
Nonvested, December 31, 2012	37,860	19.34

(b) The table summarizes all stock option activity during 2012

	Shares (thousands)	Weighted-average exercise price per share ($)	Weighted-average remaining contractual term (years)	Aggregate intrinsic value (millions)
Outstanding, December 31, 2011	429,553	25.31		
Granted	57,919	21.04		
Exercised	37,160	15.98		
Forfeited	6,881	19.12		

	Shares (thousands)	Weighted-average exercise price per share ($)	Weighted-average remaining contractual term (years)	Aggregate intrinsic value (millions)
Canceled	60,476	35.96		
Outstanding, December 31, 2012	382,955	24.00	5.0	1,230
Vested and expected to vest December 31, 2012	375,102	24.10	4.9	1,183
Exercisable, December 31, 2012	225,829	27.32	2.8	308

(c) The table summarizes all PPS activity during 2012, with the shares representing the maximum award that could be achieved

	Shares (thousands)	Weighted-average intrinsic value per share ($)
Nonvested, December 31, 2011	—	—
Granted	3,964	21.03
Vested	2	22.42
Forfeited	220	23.18
Nonvested, December 31, 2012	3,742	25.08

The accounting policies of pensions and other post-employment benefits (OPEB) and required tables for Pfizer (from Pfizer's 2012 10-k) are presented in Tables A3.3 to A3.6. Pfizer's accounting policies are described in Note 1 and 1-P covers pensions and OPEB. Like most very big older public corporations, Pfizer has both defined benefit and defined contribution plans, as well as supplementary executive retirement plans. The remaining tables indicate that there are defined benefit plans both in the United States and internationally.

Table A3.4 covers the calculation associated with pension expense for fiscal year 2012 called *net periodic benefit costs*, which was $458 million for U.S. plans in 2012 and $279 million for international plans. Executives

Table A3.3 Accounting policies for Pfizer, 2012

Pension and Postretirement Benefit Plans (Note P)

The majority of our employees worldwide are covered by defined benefit pension plans, defined contribution plans, or both. In the United States, we have both qualified and supplemental (nonqualified) defined benefit plans, as well as other postretirement benefit plans, consisting primarily of health care and life insurance for retirees. Beginning on January 1, 2011, for employees hired in the United States and Puerto Rico after December 31, 2010, we no longer offer a defined benefit plan and, instead, offer an enhanced benefit under our defined contribution plan. On May 8, 2012, we announced to employees that as of January 1, 2018, Pfizer will transition its U.S. and Puerto Rico employees from its defined benefit plans to an enhanced defined contribution savings plan. We recognize the overfunded or underfunded status of each of our defined benefit plans as an asset or liability on our consolidated balance sheet. The obligations are generally measured at the actuarial present value of all benefits attributable to employee service rendered, as provided by the applicable benefit formula. Our pension and other postretirement obligations may include assumptions such as long-term rate of return on plan assets, expected employee turnover, and participant mortality. For our pension plans, the obligation may also include assumptions as to future compensation levels. For our other postretirement benefit plans, the obligation may include assumptions as to the expected cost of providing the health care and life insurance benefits, as well as the extent to which those costs are shared with the employee or others (such as governmental programs). Plan assets are measured at fair value. Net periodic benefit costs are recognized, as required, into *cost of sales, selling, informational and administrative expenses*, and *research and development expenses*, as appropriate.

Amounts recorded for pension and postretirement benefit plans can result from a complex series of judgments about future events and uncertainties and can rely heavily on estimates and assumptions. For information about the risks associated with estimates and assumptions, see *Note 1C. Basis of Presentation and Significant Accounting Policies: Estimates and Assumptions.*

Table A3.4 Pension/OPEB note, Pfizer 2012 10-k: components of net periodic benefit costs and changes in other comprehensive loss (Table A3.4 provides the annual cost and changes in other comprehensive loss for our benefit plans)

(Millions of dollars)	Year ended December 31,											
	Pension plans									Postretirement plans		
	U.S. qualified			U.S. supplemental (nonqualified)			International					
	2012	2011	2010	2012	2011	2010	2012	2011	2010	2012	2011	2010
Service cost	357	351	347	35	36	28	215	243	224	68	68	79
Interest cost	697	734	740	62	72	77	406	443	418	182	195	211
Expected return on plan assets	(983)	(871)	(782)	—	—	—	(424)	(437)	(425)	(46)	(35)	(31)
Amortization of:												
Actuarial losses	306	145	151	41	36	29	93	86	67	33	17	15
Prior service credits	(10)	(8)	2	(3)	(3)	(2)	(7)	(5)	(4)	(49)	(53)	(38)
Curtailments and settlements—net	83	95	(52)	24	23	1	(9)	—	(3)	(65)	(68)	(23)
Special termination benefits	8	23	73	30	26	180	5	5	6	6	3	19
Net periodic benefit costs	458	469	479	189	190	313	279	335	283	129	127	232
Changes in Other comprehensive loss	461	1,879	260	110	36	117	759	(365)	152	267	421	(183)
Total amount recognized in comprehensive income	919	2,348	739	299	226	430	1,038	(30)	435	396	548	49

earned an additional $189 million for the year. The major costs were service cost and interest cost. Service costs represent the increase in pension obligations caused by employee services performed for the year ($357 million for the U.S. plans). This is an actuarial estimate based on the present value of additional pension benefits earned. Interest costs represent the time value of money, and the present value of the obligations must be adjusted because the employees are one year closer to retirement. The discount rate used will be somewhat arbitrary but typically determined (at least in part) by the actuary. The cost was a substantial $697 million, almost double the service cost. Pfizer used a discount rate of 5.1 percent for U.S. plans.

The expected return on plan assets represents the long-term estimate of the return on earnings assets (not the actual return, which is described later). Because actual earnings can be extremely volatile on an annual basis, the idea was a forecast longer-term approach usually based on previous experience. The calculation is the beginning balance of plan assets at fair value times the expected return percentage. Pfizer used an 8.5 percent expected return for U.S. plan assets, resulting in an expected return of $983 for U.S. plans. This is a negative pension expense; that is, it reduces pension expense. Other amortization adjustments include prior service costs, because pension amendments can change the total obligations and these additional obligations are amortized over time. Actuarial gains and losses are unexpected changes in the fair value of plan assets and other changes associated with modifications of assumptions.

Table A3.5 is the calculation of the net pension asset or obligation position recording on the balance sheet, the funded status. Funded status is the fair value of plan assets less projected benefit obligation (PBO). The table shows the beginning PBO for the year plus/minus the various changes (basically the amounts in Table A3.2 for calculating pension expense plus/minus changes in assumptions and other amounts), which equals ending PBO. From that is subtracted fair value of plan asset, calculated as beginning balance plus/minus gains/losses on assets, less pension benefits paid and other adjustments. Pfizer had PBO for U.S. plans at year-end of $16,268 million and plan assets at fair value of $12,540 million. The difference was the funded status of negative $3,728 million. That is, the U.S. plans were underfunded by $3,728 million, a net liability. The total funded status for all pension plans was a negative $7,915 million—all were underfunded.

Table A3.5 Pension/OPEB note, Pfizer 2012 10-k: obligations and funded status (Table A3.5 provides an analysis of the changes in our benefit obligations, plan assets, and funded status of our benefit plans)

(Millions of dollars)	Year ended December 31,						Postretirement plans	
	Pension plans							
	U.S. qualified		U.S. supplemental (nonqualified)		International			
	2012	2011	2012	2011	2012	2011	2012	2011
Change in benefit obligation								
Benefit obligation, beginning	14,835	13,035	1,431	1,401	8,891	8,965	3,900	3,582
Service cost	357	351	35	36	215	243	68	68
Interest cost	697	734	62	72	406	443	182	195
Employee contributions	—	—	—	—	9	12	58	45
Plan amendments	—	73	—	9	1	4	24	28
Changes in actuarial assumptions and other	1,926	1,808	252	111	1,232	516	259	300
Foreign exchange impact	—	—	—	—	80	304	1	—
Acquisitions	1	56	1	—	71	3	—	14
Curtailments	605	97	80	10	101	121	11	17
Settlements	485	476	121	128	33	56	—	—
Special termination benefits	8	23	30	26	5	5	6	3

(Continued)

Table A3.5 Pension/OPEB note, Pfizer 2012 10-k: obligations and funded status (Table A3.5 provides an analysis of the changes in our benefit obligations, plan assets, and funded status of our benefit plans) (Continued)

	Year ended December 31,						Postretirement plans	
	Pension plans							
	U.S. qualified		U.S. supplemental (nonqualified)		International			
(Millions of dollars)	2012	2011	2012	2011	2012	2011	2012	2011
Benefits paid	464	526	61	68	387	395	274	296
Benefit obligation, ending	16,268	14,835	1,549	1,431	10,227	8,891	4,165	3,900
Change in plan assets								
Fair value of plan assets, beginning	12,005	10,596	—	—	6,953	6,542	422	414
Actual gain on plan assets	1,464	398	—	—	668	176	85	9
Company contributions	20	1,969	182	196	383	475	353	250
Employee contributions	—	—	—	—	9	12	58	45
Foreign exchange impact	—	—	—	—	35	197	—	—
Acquisitions	—	44	—	—	31	2	—	—
Settlements	485	476	121	128	33	56	—	—
Benefits paid	464	526	61	68	387	395	274	296
Fair value of plan assets, ending	12,540	12,005	—	—	7,589	6,953	644	422
Funded status—plan assets less than benefit obligation	3,728	2,830	1,549	1,431	2,638	1,938	3,521	3,478

Table A3.6 summarized the plan assets of Pfizer's plans. Only the U.S. and international plans have earning assets, primarily because of tax rules; that is, the contributions to purchase plan assets are deductible for these *qualified plans*, but not for SERPs. The table shows the distribution of assets into cash, equities, and fixed income. Fair value is measured by *level*, with level 1 based on market values. Stocks, bonds, and other assets traded on a public exchange have an easily determined closing value at year-end. Other asset values must be estimated, with level 3 often based on *mark-to-model*, subject to model assumptions and potential manipulation. The total ending value is used in the Table A3.5 calculations of funded status.

OPEB accounting and disclosures are similar to pensions, and pension and OPEB calculations are often presented in the same tables, as is the case with Pfizer in Tables A3.1 to A3.4. Table A3.1 adds additional information on the OPEB plans, including the importance of estimating obligations of providing health care and life insurance. The last columns of Tables A3.2 to A3.4 are the OPEB calculations. Table A3.2 is the calculation of OPEB expense for 2012, $548 million, with component definitions similar to pensions. Table A3.3 summarizes the calculation of the funded status of OPEB, which was underfunded by $3,478 million. A major factor in the relatively large underfunding was the small investment in assets ($644 million), as with supplemental executive retirement plans (SERPs) because of tax rules that treat the investments as non-tax deductibles. Also small, the investments are summarized in Table A3.6.

Table A3.6 Pension/OPEB note, Pfizer 2012 10-k: plan assets (Table A3.6 provides the components of plan assets)

(Millions of dollars)	As of December 31, 2012	Fair value			As of December 31, 2011	Fair value		
		Level 1	Level 2	Level 3		Level 1	Level 2	Level 3
U.S. qualified pension plans								
Cash and cash equivalents	368	—	368	—	2,111	—	2,111	—
Equity securities:								
Global equity securities	3,536	3,519	17	—	2,522	2,509	12	1
Equity commingled funds	2,215	—	2,215	—	1,794	—	1,794	—
Debt securities:								
Fixed income commingled funds	943	—	943	—	870	—	870	—
Government bonds	1,093	—	1,093	—	808	—	805	3
Corporate debt securities	2,414	—	2,411	3	1,971	—	1,966	5
Other investments:								
Private equity funds	866	—	—	866	920	—	—	920
Insurance contracts	348	—	348	—	353	—	353	—
Other	757	—	—	757	656	—	—	656
Total	12,540	3,519	7,395	1,626	12,005	2,509	7,911	1,585

(Millions of dollars)	Fair value				Fair value			
	As of December 31, 2012	Level 1	Level 2	Level 3	As of December 31, 2011	Level 1	Level 2	Level 3
International pension plans								
Cash and cash equivalents	299	—	299	—	299	—	299	—
Equity securities:								
Global equity securities	1,723	1,638	85	—	1,513	1,432	81	—
Equity commingled funds	2,194	—	2,194	—	1,966	—	1,966	—
Debt securities:								
Fixed income commingled funds	825	—	825	—	785	—	785	—
Government bonds	914	—	914	—	956	—	956	—
Corporate debt securities	613	—	613	—	536	—	536	—
Other investments:								
Private equity funds	110	—	14	96	55	—	4	51
Insurance contracts	465	—	117	348	433	—	67	366
Other	446	—	57	389	410	—	62	348
Total	7,589	1,638	5,118	833	6,953	1,432	4,756	765

(Continued)

Table A3.6 Pension/OPEB note, Pfizer 2012 10-k: plan assets (Table A3.6 provides the components of plan assets) (Continued)

(Millions of dollars)	Fair value				Fair value			
	As of December 31, 2012	Level 1	Level 2	Level 3	As of December 31, 2011	Level 1	Level 2	Level 3
U.S. postretirement plans								
Cash and cash equivalents	28	—	28	—	19	—	19	—
Equity securities: Global equity securities	79	79	—	—	24	24	—	—
Equity commingled funds	50	—	50	—	17	—	17	—
Debt securities:	20	—	20	—	8	—	8	—
Fixed income commingled funds								
Government bonds	25	—	25	—	8	—	8	—
Corporate debt securities	55	—	55	—	19	—	19	—
Other investments:	350	—	350	—	312	—	312	—
Insurance contracts								
Other	37	—	37	—	15	—	15	—
Total	644	79	565	—	422	24	398	—

Timeline

Executive Compensation Events

Bonus Plans	1902	Both Bethlehem Steel and United States Steel first paid cash bonuses to executives.
Pujo Committee Hearings	1913	Congressional hearings on the "Money Trust" documented many of the illicit activities of Wall Street. Reform legislation followed.
Sixteenth Amendment. Federal Reserve, Federal Trade Commission, Clayton Act	1913–14	Substantial federal reform legislation followed the Pujo Hearings, including new anti-trust and related legislation, the creation of the Federal Reserve System and Federal Trade Commission, and a permanent federal income tax. A major rationale for a progressive income tax was the incredible income inequality, typically associated with the "robber barons."
Stock Maneuvering and Speculation	1920s	It was anything goes at the New York Stock Exchange, including insider trading, stock pools for price manipulation, and stock pyramiding. Stock prices fueled by speculation and margin buying created a bubble which collapsed at the end of 1929, ultimately resulting in the Great Depression of the 1930s.
Million Dollar Salary	1927–29	Charles Mitchell, president and chairman of National City Bank, received over $1 million a year in compensation over these years. This was discovered during the Pecora Commission hearings.
Million Dollar Salary	1929	W.R. Grace, president of Bethlehem Steel, was paid over $1.6 million in compensation, triggering public outrage after disclosure associated with a lawsuit.
Stock Market Crash	1929	The market crashed in October 1929 after years of speculation and inflated stock prices; the Great Depression followed, largely because of inept government actions.
Railroad Executive Compensation	1932	Interstate Commerce Commission (ICC) required all railroads to disclose executive compensation over $10,000; The Reconstruction Finance Corporation (RFC) required railroads receiving government help to reduce executive compensation.

Pecora Commission	1932–34	Congressional hearings on the causes of the market crash and Great Depression, documenting the abusive practices of business and Wall Street. New Deal Legislation followed.
Federal Investigation	1933	Federal Trade Commission studied executive compensation of firms listed on the New York Stock Exchange and New York Curb Exchange (later the American Stock Exchange) from 1928–33. Compensation peaked in 1929–30, then fell substantially by 1932.
Securities Act	1933	Based on the findings of massive wrongdoing on Wall Street and at corporations, the Securities Act under FDR's New Deal established increased federal regulations of securities markets and the public firms that traded on them (initially under the Federal Trade Commission).
Securities Exchange Act	1934	Created the SEC to regulate securities markets and provide adequate disclosures of public corporations' finances. The Act defined insiders and required insiders to file stock ownership and changes in ownership with the SEC.
SEC Disclosures of Executive Compensation	1934– present	Required annual disclosures included the compensation of the top corporate executives, initially the compensation received by the three highest-paid executives. Specific disclosure requirements changed over the years, but executive compensation has been disclosed every year since then.
Book on Executive Pay	1938	John Baker publishes *Executive Salaries and Bonus Plans*, analyzing the FTC data for 1928–33 and additional data from SEC disclosures from 1934–1936.
Creation of Committee on Accounting Procedures	1938	CAP was created to established "generally accepted accounting principles (GAAP), using Accounting Research Bulletins. Fifty-one ARBs were issues over 20 years (1938–59). These represented many of the fundamental accounting standards still in use (although the particulars have changed over time).
Stabilization Act	1942	Froze wages and salaries (expired in 1946, after World War II ended).
Pay-as-you-Go Act	1943	Introduces income tax withholding from each paycheck, making high tax rates more palatable.

Individual Income Tax Act	1944	Set the top rate at 94%, but capital gains rate stayed at 25%.
Revenue Act	1950	Created "restricted stock options:" not taxed until exercised options were sold and then at the capital gains rate.
Salary Stabilization Board	1951	Board established during Korean War to put a cap on wages; a 6% cap was put in place on executive pay. Disbanded in 1952.
Revenue Act	1954	Limited the exercise term of stock options to 10 years and allowed option repricing to lower the exercise price if stock price declined after the original grant date.
Accounting Principles Board	1959	The APB replaced the CAP, using new procedures but with many of problems of the previous organization.
First Golden Parachute	1961	Strategy used by creditors to oust Howard Hughes from Trans World Airlines, when Charles Tillinghast became chairman; use of golden parachutes expanded in 1980s as hostile takeovers increased.
Self-Employed Individuals Tax Retirement Act	1962	Established Keogh (HR-10) retirement plans for the self-employed.
Revenue Act	1964	Reduced the top individual income tax rate to 77% (later dropping to 70%). "Qualified stock options" replaced "restricted options," reducing the attractiveness of options, including the requirement that the recipient hold exercised options for three years before they could be sold and reducing the option term to five years.
Tax Reform Act	1969	Required restricted stock to be taxed when received unless subject to risk of forfeiture. Introduced a form of the alternative minimum tax (AMT).
Economic Stabilization Act	1970	Gave the president the authority to impose wage and price controls.
Forbes List	1970	*Forbes* started its annual list of public companies highest-paid executives; other publications started similar compensation surveys.
Nixon Shock	1971	Wage and price controls established as part of President Nixon's effects to combat high unemployment and interest rates. Wages and prices frozen for 90 days; after that, a 5.5% cap was placed on executive pay increases.

APB Opinion 25	1972	"Accounting for Stock Issued to Employees," establishing the "measurement date principle," valuing the stock on the first day when both the number of shares and price were known.
Financial Accounting Standards Board	1973	The FASB was established to replace the APB, with an improved process, governance, and public involvement.
Employment Retirement Income Security Act	1974	Established the individual retirement account (IRA) for employees not covered by corporate pension plans. Substantial requirements on funding and disclosures of employer pension plans.
Foreign Corrupt Practices Act	1977	After several bribery scandals of foreign officials, Act made bribery in foreign countries for business purposes illegal. It also mandated internal control requirements of public firms.
Executive Compensation Disclosures	1978	SEC required tabulated pay disclosures for top executives, including perquisites; first major overhaul of compensation disclosures.
Revenue Act	1978	Section 401(k) on cash and deferred compensation allowed a new form of defined contribution pension plan. Favorable tax treatment for deferred compensation.
Economic Recovery Act	1981	Established incentive stock options (ISOs).
Tax Reform Act	1984	Eliminated advantages of interest-free loans. Created a 20% excise tax on golden parachutes to executives and loss of corporate tax deductions above allowable amount.
Michael Eisner's Compensation	1984	Disney's CEO contract made him the highest paid CEO up to that time, rising to $57 million in 1989.
FASB Statement No. 87	1985	"Employers' Accounting for Pensions," requiring the balance sheet to reflect the net value of the plan (fair value of plan assets less accumulated pension obligations).
Tax Reform Act	1986	Major tax overhaul, dropping the top rate to 28%, including capital gains.
FASB Statement No. 106	1990	"Employers' Accounting for Post-retirement Benefits Other than Pensions," similar to pensions, with the balance sheet recording the net value (fair value of plan assets less OPEB obligations.

Jensen and Murphy Article	1990	Influential *Harvard Business Review* article promoted the use of performance-based pay for CEOs, especially the use of stock options.
SEC Rules	1991	Requires executives to hold exercised stock options at least six months before selling.
SEC Disclosures	1992	Allowed non-binding shareholders resolutions on CEO pay in the proxy statement and additional pay disclosure rules.
Revenue Reconciliation Act	1993	Top individual tax rate increased to 39.6%. Limited corporate pay deduction to executives at $1 million; performance-based pay exempted.
FASB Statement No. 123	1995	Companies given the choice of using ABP 25 accounting or using an option pricing model such as Black-Scholes to value options (option pricing model results must be disclosed in footnotes).
Taxpayer Relief Act	1997	Lowered long-term capital gains to 20%. Increased alternative minimum tax to 28%. Introduced Roth IRAs.
Michael Ovitz Severance Package	1997	Ovitz became Disney's president in 1995 and his contract included a $130 severance package which was paid when he was fired soon after.
Robert Goizueta Pay	1997	Coca-Cola CEO became the first non-owner CEO to earn more than $1 billion in total compensation (1981–97).
Enron Pay	1996–2000	Enron paid its top five executives over $500 million in total compensation.
FIN 44	1998	FASB Interpretation No. 44, "Accounting for Certain Transactions Involving Stock Compensation," required companies with underwater options that were repriced an accounting charge based on appreciation in value of the option; repricing essentially disappeared after the effective date, December 15, 1998.
Economic Growth and Tax Reconciliation Act	2001	Top corporate income tax rate reduced to 35%.
Regulation FD (Full Disclosure)	2001	SEC required increased public disclosure when companies talked to analysts and other investment insiders. Earnings announcements were required to be made publicly, usually through internet simulcasts.

Enron	2001	Enron transformed from a stogy gas pipeline company to a gas trader that claimed to be a global high tech company. This facade was maintained through fraud, including the widespread use of special purpose entities, market values, derivatives, and deceptive use of trading profits. Possibly the biggest business scandal in American history; several executives were jailed.
WorldCom	2002	Large telecom company temporarily avoided failure when actual profits collapsed by simple fraud: recorded operating expenses as capital assets—some $11 billion. Several executives were jailed including CEO Bernie Ebbers.
Adelphia	2002	Cable TV empire used accounting fraud in part to compensate for corporate governance violations to benefit Regas family members. Adelphia went bankrupt and several Regas's (all on the board) went to jail.
Sarbanes-Oxley Act	2002	After the Enron and WorldCom scandals and all the rest, Congress passed financial reform, including new rules on corporate governance, internal control, auditing, and the creation of the Public Company Accounting Oversight Board.
Richard Grasso Resignation	2003	CEO of New York Stock Exchange forced out after disclosing he received pension benefits of almost $140 million. (SEC then required companies to disclose actuarial value of pension benefits.)
Fannie Mae	2004	Fraudulent accounting practices to produce excessive executive pay; earnings restated and executives fired.
FASB Statement No. 123R	2004	Required companies to use option pricing model (such as Black-Scholes) to value options and record compensation as an expense, effective in 2006.
SEC Investigation of GE over CEO Disclosures	2004	General Electric settled suit on massive retirement package for former CEO Jack Welch (which was far greater than disclosed in the proxy statement).
SEC Charges Companies on Disclosures	2005	SEC sued Tyson Foods and Tyco over failures to disclose substantial executive perquisites. Tighter disclosure rules on perks followed.

Fired CEOs	2005–6	Several high-profile and high-paid CEOs received huge termination packages after being ousted, including Pfizer's Henry McKinnell ($190 million), Hewlett-Packard's Carly Fiorina ($21 million), Viacom's Tom Freston ($85 million), and Sovereign Bank's Jay Sidhu ($44 million).
Stock Option Backdating	2006	The SEC discovered that dozens of companies were backdating stock option awards to increase executive compensation. Several executives were prosecuted. A number of other stock options manipulations were uncovered including exercise backdating, spring-loading and speed vesting.
Congressional Hearings	2007	Compensation consultants accused of being complicit in excessive executive compensation awards; SEC required increased disclosures of consultants' role.
Sub-prime Loan Scandal	2007–8	Mortgage lending became a massive manipulation scheme involving predatory lending practices, structured finance of mortgages manipulated to appear high quality, and widespread speculation. The scandals started to unravel in 2007 as housing prices declined.
Bear Stearns	2008	Failing investment bank Bear Stearns was acquired by J.P. Morgan after the Fed agreed to a $30 billion bailout.
Fannie Mae, Freddie Mack	2008	These large government-sponsored enterprises were put into conservatorship by the federal government after numerous accounting scandals and insolvency.
Merrill Lynch	2008	Investment bank Merrill Lynch was acquired by Bank of America (B of A); a move B of A soon regretted and B of A CEO Ken Lewis was soon fired.
Lehman Brothers Bankruptcy	2008	Investment bank Lehman failed after federal government could not (or refused) a bailout, the biggest bankruptcy in American history.
American Insurance Group	2008	Insurance giant AIG was bailed out by the Fed, some $185 billion, after gigantic losses associated with selling credit default swaps.

Troubled Asset Relief Program	2008	After Treasury and Fed prodding, Congress passed TARP, which provided billions of dollars of capital to failing banks. The bill was originally designed to bail out mortgagees, which happened only to a limited extent. Executive pay reduced for companies bailed out under TARP.
SEC Disclosure Rules	2009	SEC required corporations to disclose fees charged by executive compensation consultants when the consultants were paid over $120,000 for other services.
Pay Czar	2009	Treasury Department Special Master had responsibility over the compensation of the 25 top executive in each company receiving TARP funding.
Dodd-Frank Act	2010	Congress eventually passed the massive Financial Reform bill in 2010: "to promote the financial stability of the United States by improving accountability and transparency in the financial system, to end 'too big to fail,' to protect the American taxpayer by ending bailouts, to protect consumers from abusive financial services practices, and for other purposes." The potential effectiveness has been debated ever since. Stockholder vote (non-binding) required on executive pay packages.
Financial Crisis Inquiry Report	2011	The Financial Crisis Inquiry Commission issued its final report at the start of 2011 on the causes of the 2008 financial crisis. The report was not unanimous and split along party lines.
Annual CEO Compensation	2013	Two CEOs received over $1 billion in total compensation in 2012: Mark Zuckerberg of Facebook, $2.3 billion (mainly because of options exercised); Richard Kinder of Kinder Morgan, $1.1 billion (mainly because of shares vested). The top ten highest paid CEOs all received over $100 million in total compensation.
Sheryl Sandberg, billionaire	2014	Sheryl Sandberg, COO of Facebook, became the first non-owner female executive to accumulate $1 billion in wealth mainly through stock options and accumulated shares.

Laws And Regulations: Executive Compensation (Including Tax)

Federal Tax Act	1862	First federal income tax (to fund the Civil War), repealed in 1872.
Tariff Act	1909	Income tax of 1% on corporate profits over $5,000.
16th Amendment	1913	Allowed Congress to levy an income tax.
Underwood-Simmons Tariff Act	1913	Established a progressive income tax on individuals; maximum 7% over $500,000.
Revenue Act	1917	Top tax rate 77% on income over $200,000 (during World War I).
Revenue Act	1920	Top tax rate reduced to 50% over $200,000.
Revenue Act	1921	Introduced capital gains rates to encourage investment, initially 12.5%.
Revenue Act	1925	Top tax rate reduced to 25% over $100,000.
Revenue Act	1932	Raised top tax rate on individuals to 77%.
Securities Act	1933	Required executives to hold restricted stock at least two years before selling it.
Securities Exchange Act	1934	Defined insiders and required insiders to file stock ownership and changes in ownership with the SEC.
Stabilization Act	1942	World War II law to freeze wages but allowed additional fringe benefits.
Current Tax Payment Act	1943	Income tax withholding started; prior to that, income tax was an annual payment.
Individual Income Tax Act	1944	Top tax rate set at 94% over $200,000; capital gains at 25%.
Revenue Act	1950	Introduces the concept of "restricted stock options" taxed at capital gains rate.
Self-Employed Individuals Tax Retirement Act	1962	Established Keogh (HR-10) retirement plans for the self-employed.
Revenue Act	1964	Created qualified stock options, making replacing restricted stock options less attractive; top tax rate reduced to 77%.
Revenue Act	1965	Top tax rate reduced to 70%.
Tax Reform Act	1969	Required restricted stock to be taxed when received unless subject to risk of forfeiture. Introduced a form of alternative minimum tax. Long-term capital gain rate increased to 35%; alternative minimum tax introduced.

Economic Stabilization Act	1970	Gave the president the authority to impose wage and price controls. Used by President Nixon in 1971 and President Carter in 1978.
APB Opinion 25	1972	Accounting Principles Board Opinion "Accounting for Stock Issued to Employees," to determine compensation expenses based on "intrinsic value" and no expense recorded as long as exercise price was equal to (or more than) grant-date market price.
Employment Retirement Income Security Act (ERISA)	1974	Established the individual retirement Account (IRA) for employees not covered by corporate pension plans. Substantial requirements on funding and disclosures of employer pension plans.
Tax Reform Act	1976	Eliminated qualified stock options and increased eligibility for employee stock purchase plans.
Revenue Act	1978	Section 401(k) on cash and deferred compensation allowed a new form of defined contribution pension plan. Favorable tax treatment for deferred compensation. Capital gains rate reduce to 28%.
Economic Recovery Act	1981	Established incentive stock options (ISOs). Capital gains rate reduced to 20%. Top individual rate reduced to 50%.
Tax Reform Act	1984	Eliminated advantages of interest-free loans. Created a 20% excise tax on golden parachutes to executives and loss of corporate tax deduction above allowable amount.
Tax Reform Act	1986	Major tax overhaul, including lowering the top income tax rate to 28%, raising capital gains rate to 28%, and raised alternative minimum tax to 21%.
Omnibus Budget Reconciliation Act	1990	Increased top individual rate to 31% and alternative minimum tax to 24%.
Revenue Reconciliation Act	1993	Raised top individual tax rate to 39.6%, maintained the capital gains rate at 28%, and raised the alternative minimum tax to 28%. Section 162(m) limited corporate pay deduction to executives to $1 million unless linked to company performance.
FASB Statement No. 123	1995	Replaced APBO 25, recommending but not requiring companies to record compensation expense for options based on option pricing models.

Taxpayer Relief Act	1997	Lowered long-term capital gains rate to 20%; increase alternative minimum tax to 28%. Introduced Roth IRAs.
Tax Code Changes	1999	Congress attempted to limit golden parachutes by limiting tax deductibility of "change-in-control" payments (by 1999 about 70% of the largest 1,000 corporations had golden parachute agreements).
Economic Growth and Tax Reconciliation Act	2001	Phase-in of tax cuts, including elimination of estate taxes in 2010. Top individual rate reduced to 35%; capital gains to 15% and dividend income to 15%.
Sarbanes-Oxley Act	2002	Financial reform act following Enron and other financial scandals, including substantial regulation of corporate governance.
American Jobs Creation Act	2004	After senior Enron executives were allowed to withdraw millions from deferred compensation accounts just before declaring bankruptcy in 2002, Congress limited timing flexibility in withdrawing deferred compensation.
FASB Statement No. 123R	2004	Requires companies to record compensation expense for options at grant date based on an option pricing model.
Dodd-Frank Act	2010	Financial reform bill following the subprime meltdown, which includes provisions impacting on compensation.
Tax Relief Act	2010	Increased top individual tax rate to 39.6%.

Glossary

Terms	Definitions
10-K	Annual report for the ending fiscal year describing the financial position and operating results of the company, including financial statements.
10-Q	Quarterly financial report issued by public corporations to the Securities and Exchange Commission (SEC).
8-K	Special report issued to the SEC to describe material-specific event, such as a change in auditor.
Accounting Fraud	Intentional misstatements of financial information for personal gain.
Accounting Standards	Financial accounting rules and procedures issued by authorized bodies such as the Financial Accounting Standards Board (FASB).
Adverse Selection	Poor market decisions make because one party does not have the information to make an efficient decision (i.e., information asymmetry).
Agency Cost	Costs incurred by agents related to information asymmetries, adverse selection, or moral hazard.
Agency Theory	Economics theory that all contracts have a principal and an agent; principals attempt to write efficient contracts to maximize their own interests and minimize agency and transaction costs.
Aggressive Accounting	Accounting techniques and choices to manipulate reported revenues, expenses, earnings, and financial position to result in a specific outcome (such as earnings per share to meet analysts' expectations).
Antidilutive	Procedures to reduce the number of shares of stock outstanding such as buying back company shares (treasury stock).
Asset	Item owned that has probable future economic benefits.
Audit (or Financial Audit)	A substantial review of the items and records of a corporation by a licensed professional to ensure that the financial records are presented in accordance with generally accepted accounting principles.
Backdating (stock options)	Stock options are generally issued on the grant date at the market price; in some companies, an earlier date was used when the stock price (also the exercise price) was lower, allowing the holder to increase income when the options were exercised.

Terms	Definitions
Balance Sheet	A financial statement showing the assets, liabilities, and equity of an organization as of a specific date.
Base Pay	Fixed cash salary paid to employees without regard to performance.
Bear Market	A substantial stock market downturn, usually defined as more than 20%.
Big Four	The major accounting firms in the United States and much of the world: PricewaterhouseCoopers, Deloitte & Touche, Ernst & Young, and KPMG. Previously the Big Eight.
Black-Scholes	A mathematical model to determine the value of an option, the first of many pricing models that allowed derivatives to be accurately priced.
Bonus (Salary)	Cash (or stock) paid in addition to base salary usually based on performance such as corporate earnings.
Bounded Rationality	Decision makers are limited by the information available, decision-making ability, and time constraints, resulting in seeking satisfying decision making such as rules of thumb.
Bubble	A period of time when asset prices (especially stocks and real estate) trade at substantially more than their fundamental values.
Bull Market	A substantial stock market upturn, usually over 20%.
Business Cycle	The periodic ups and downs of an economy, including boom times and busts (usually recessions).
Call (or Call Option)	A derivative allowing the buyer to buy a particular asset (e.g., stock, oil) at a stated price during some time period.
Capital	Wealth in the form of money, financial securities, real estate and other real property.,
Capital Markets	Organizations or mechanisms to trade securities (including derivatives) and commodities, where prices are based on supply and demand.
Capitalism	An economic system that used private ownership or production and distribution, with prices established by market mechanisms.
Capture Theory	Economic theory that regulatory agencies are "captured" by the industry they are supposed to regulate; that is, they work in the interests of the industry rather than the public.
Civil Law	In Europe, based on Roman law and legal compilations to produce comprehensive legal systems. Some 150 countries exercise some form of civil law.
Clawbacks	Contractual provisions in which pay or benefits previously given out are returned to the corporation.

Terms	Definitions
Cognitive Capture	Regulators who have the mindset associated with the industry they are supposed to regulate, putting the interests of the industry above that of the public.
Collateral	Securities or physical assets pledged by a borrower to protect the creditor in case of loan default.
Common Law	An English legal system based on judicial interpretations of customs and rulings by monarchs, emphasizing legal precedent. Perhaps 80 countries use some form of common law including the United States.
Conflict of Interest	Circumstance where an individual can achieve a personal gain based on his or her inside information or official capacity.
Corporate Governance	The structure in place to oversee corporations or other organizations by the board of directors and others.
Credit Risk	The likelihood that a company will default on debt or declare bankruptcy.
Creeping Takeaways	Slowly reducing employee benefits, such as pensions and health care.
Debt and Leverage	Debt accumulated by an organization or individual and the analysis of risk related to relative debt to equity.
Deferred Compensation	Compensation that will be paid in a future period, usually to shift income to reduce taxes or maximize individual wealth in other ways, such as tax-sheltered plans.
Defined Benefit Plan	Retirement plan paying periodic annuity payments based on some formula, such as years of service and final salary.
Defined Contribution Plan	Retirement plan based on employee and/or employee contributions to a fund (the 401(k) is the most common), with no further obligation by the employer.
Deregulation	Reducing or eliminating government regulations, especially related to business. Presumably, market forces become more significant as deregulation increases.
Derivatives	These are contracts derived from existing securities or other contracts, including futures, options, and swaps.
Disclosure	Usually defined as the details of accounts and transactions as detailed in the notes to the annual report.
Discount Rates	Theoretical interest rate to determine the "real" amount of future payoffs or obligations, such as the obligations of defined benefit pension plans.
Dodd-Frank Bill	Federal legislation of 2010 designed to fix the banking problems associated with the Subprime Meltdown of 2008.

Terms	Definitions
Double-entry Accounting	The recording of debits and credits that equal in every journal entry and that up to the equation: assets = liabilities + owners' equity.
Dow-Jones Industrial Average (DOW)	An index of the weighted stock prices of 30 major industrial firms used a measure of stock market performance.
Earnings Management	Process of using operating changes and discretionary accounting alternatives to move earnings to a desired outcome, such as consensus analyst forecasts.
Earnings Manipulation	Process of using aggressive accounting methods to move accounting earnings to some outcome, usually based on illicit/unethical practices.
Earnings Per Share (EPS)	Net income divided by weighted-average number of shares outstanding (basic EPS) or adjusted to consider items such as stock options that potentially increase shares outstanding (diluted EPS).
Earnings Quality	The relative extent to which earnings represent financial reality, usually associated with full disclosure and conservative accounting practices.
Earnings Restatements	Accounting revision to a previously issued (and audited) annual report that has to be corrected. Often used as an indicator of accounting manipulation.
Economic Consequences	Intended or unintended results of specific actions such as a change in regulations or new financial product.
Economic Regulation	Rules and regulations (usually by government) that limit market behavior, such as pollution control, bank deposit levels, or financial reporting requirements.
Economies of Scale	Size advantage of large organizations through lower unit costs (especially by spreading fixed costs over more units) and facilitating distribution.
Efficient Contracting	Ability to write contracts to minimize transaction costs and maximize principal's income.
Efficient Contracting	Economic theory that contracts in a "perfect market" are efficient.
Efficient Markets	Economic theory stating that the information available in free markets is reflected almost immediately in prices.
Employee Benefits	Compensation in addition to salary usually paid to full-time and perhaps to part-time employees, including health and other types of insurance, pension and other retirement benefits, and so on.
Enforcement Action	Legal action taken by the SEC based on the violation of SEC rules and regulations by corporations and other entities under SEC jurisdiction.

Terms	Definitions
Ethics	Moral principles in conduct by individuals and organizations.
Executive	Key corporate official based on job title, salary, job grade, or some combination of these.
Executive Compensation	Pay to top executives based on base pay, bonuses, stock-based compensation, perquisites, and other benefits.
Expert Networks	Research organization that connect investors (e.g., private equity and hedge funds) with industry experts.
Extrinsic Motivation	Performing an activity to obtain an outcome determined from the outside, including performance-based pay.
Fair Value Accounting	Valuing assets and liabilities based on current market price or other available indicator of current value if market price is not available.
FASB Codification	All FASB standards were codified in 2009 and listed under topics; for example, "200" covers presentation, with the balance sheet under 210 and the income statement 225.
Federal Reserve System	Central bank of the United States, created in 1914, with jurisdiction over monetary policy and oversight of bank holding companies and other entities.
Financial Accounting Standards Board (FASB)	Private sector authoritative body (according to the SEC) with responsibility to establish generally accepted accounting principles (GAAP) in the United States. Established in 1973 to replace the Accounting Principles Board.
Financial Analyst	Financial specialists using fundamental analysis of accounting information to forecast future corporate earnings and make buy/sell recommendations.
Financial Audit	An external review of financial reports by licensed professionals to state that financial statements are prepared in accordance with generally accepted accounting principles.
Forwards and Futures	Derivative contracts for the seller to deliver an asset (for cash or other considerations) at a specific future date and specific price; futures are traded on organized exchanges.
Fraud	Intentional deception used for personal gain; illicit and often illegal.
Free Rider Problem	Using goods and services without paying for them.
Funded Status	The net position of defined benefit pension plans, defined as the fair value of plan assets less pension benefit obligations.
Generally Accepted Accounting Principles (GAAP)	Accounting standards established by the FASB and predecessor bodies with authoritative support of the SEC.

Terms	Definitions
Gini Coefficient	Index of inequality (from 0 to 1) used to measure wealth or income distributions, named after Italian sociologist Corrado Gini.
Golden Handcuffs	Financial incentives to retain employees or limit certain actions such as stock options that do not vest for several years or non-compete clause.
Golden Parachute	Contract that gives an executive substantial benefits if an executive is terminated (usually because the company was acquired—called "change in control benefits"); also excessive CEO severance package.
Great Depression	Substantial worldwide economic downturn in the 1930s; a recession and stock crash in 1929 was turned into a major depression by counterproductive governmental actions, especially the Federal Reserve's handling of monetary policy.
Gross Domestic Product (GDP)	A measure of overall economic activity measured by the market value of all final goods and services produced within a given year.
Human Capital	Knowledge, background, experience, and other abilities of the workforce, either at the firm or macro level.
Illiquidity	Lack of cash (or other assets) to meet obligations as they come due.
Income Statement	Financial statement used to measure operating performance based on revenues, expenses, gains, and losses.
Information Asymmetry	Information differences between a buyer and seller, usually stated in economics as an agency problem between the principal (with limited information) and the agent (with the necessary information); resulting in a "veil of ignorance" by the principal leading to inferior decisions.
Insolvency	Negative equity; situation where liabilities exceed assets, usually associated with a failing company.
Interlocking Boards	Executives from competing companies (including banks, usually representing borrowers) sat on each other's board of directors.
Internal Revenue Service (IRS)	Federal agency within the Treasury Department responsible for federal income tax collection and other revenue services.
In-the-money Options	Stock options where the current value of the stock is higher than the options exercise price.
Intrinsic Motivation	People motivated by internal factors; the driver, the interest, or enjoyment of the task itself based on factors under their own control.
Kuznets Curve	Graph based on economist Simon Kuznets' theory of a natural economic inequality as a country develops; inequality increases initially but decreases as the economy matures.

Terms	Definitions
Labor Economics	The analysis of the market for wage labor, usually based on a neoclassical framework of demand and supply of labor—and labor as one of the major factors of production.
Legal Corruption	Legal, but of questionable ethics, actions for private gain such as lobbying or campaign contributions.
Liquidity	Ability of an individual or organization to pay its obligations as they come due.
Loss Averse	Preference for avoiding losses compared to acquiring gains.
Making the Number	Ability of a corporation to meet analysts' expectations, usually based on quarterly consensus earnings per share forecast.
Marshall Effect	The rise in income of those with extraordinary ability relative to those with moderate ability, named after economist Alfred Marshall.
Misery Index	A measure of stagflation, adding the unemployment rate to the inflation rate. The misery index remained over 10% from 1973 to 1985.
Monopoly Power	The market power of a monopolist to set prices and output, independent of competitive pressures.
Moral Hazard	Potential of individuals or organizations to take increased risk because they do not bear the full costs of failure; an agency cost.
NASDAQ	National Association of Security Dealers Automated Quotations, a major stock exchange located in New York City, which replaced the over-the-counter market in 1971.
NASDAQ 100	Composite index of 100 of the largest stocks listed on NASDAQ; the index started at 100 in 1971 and peaked at 5,049 in March 2000.
New Deal	The progressive program of Franklin D. Roosevelt to combat the Great Depression, including the creation of the SEC.
NYMEX	New York Mercantile Exchange: commodities' future exchange trading, including agricultural, energy, metals, and other commodities.
NYSE	New York Stock Exchange: largest stock exchange in the world, headquartered in New York City (and the center of Wall Street), founded in 1792.
Off-Balance-Sheet Financing	Techniques used to keep assets and especially liabilities off the balance sheet, generally to understate the degree of leverage, such as special purpose entities or operating leases; a form of earnings management.
Oligopoly Power	A small number of firms within an industry has the power to dominate the market in terms of price and output.

Terms	Definitions
Opportunistic Behavior	Selfish behavior that violates ethical standards.
Optimal Contracting Theory	Economic theory studying contract arrangement to incentivize agents to maximize firm value; especially in management compensation.
Options	Derivatives that give the buyer the right to buy (call) or sell (put) specific assets, including stocks.
Other Comprehensive Income	Gains and losses that are part of stockholders' equity but not included in net income, including certain marketable securities, foreign currency translations, and pension/other post-employment benefits (OPEB) adjustments.
Other Post-Employment Benefits (OPEB)	Nonpension benefits paid to retired employees (or other terminated employees) such as health insurance.
Out-of-the-Money Options	Current value of the stock is lower than the exercise price of the options.
Pay for Performance	Setting compensation based on measures of performance such as corporate earnings; a common practices of associated with executive compensation after the Omnibus Budget Reconciliation Act of 1993.
Pay-As-You-Go	Practice of funding long-term commitments as cash payments as they come due, including pensions and other retirement benefits. This greatly understates the true liabilities of these obligations.
Pecora Commission	Senate Banking and Currency Committee investigation of the causes of the 1929 stock market crash, named for chief counsel, Ferdinand Pecora.
Pension Benefit Obligations (PBO)	Present value of the total obligations to pay employees their pension benefits as they come due.
Performance-based Compensation	Compensation based on some measure(s) of performance such as earnings or market value of stock.
Perquisites (Perks)	Essentially executive benefits available only to certain executives, which can include supplemental pension plans, additional insurance, and personal airplanes.
Phantom Stock Award	Incentive plan based on hypothetical shares with payout in cash or stock.
Plan Assets	Invested assets such as stock or bonds available to fund future defined benefit obligations of employees (recorded at fair value).
Plutocracy	An economic/political system led by the wealthiest citizens—the plutocrats.

Terms	Definitions
Principles-based Accounting Standards	Principles-based standards are conceptually based, using some set of objectives. Applying broad guidelines allows considerable judgment, although inconsistency is a potential problem.
Prior Service Cost	The present value of increased pension or OPEB benefits from amending or initial adoption of the pension/OPEB plan.
Professional Ethics	Standards of behavior expected of business professionals, including rules required for licensing and certification such as certified public accountants (CPAs).
Proxy Statement	Annual report required by the SEC to stockholders before the annual meeting describing the items to be voted on by the investors.
Public Company Accounting Oversight Board (PCAOB)	Organization created by the Sarbanes-Oxley Act of 2002 specifically required to oversee the financial audit process of public companies.
Qualified Stock Options	Replaced restricted options based on the 1964 Revenue Act, requiring recipients to hold exercised options for three years before they could be sold.
Quantitative Easing	Federal Reserve program to inject massive amounts of cash into the financial system after the collapse of Lehman Brothers.
Rent (Economic Rent)	Income paid to a factor of production (such as labor) in excess of opportunity cost, a form of "excess return."
Rent Seeking	The attempt to achieve excess return (economic rent), often by manipulation.
Reputational Risk	Relative trustworthiness; damage to the reputation of major brands such as Coca-Cola or Apple could cause substantial repercussions to market share and earnings.
Restricted Stock	Common stock not yet fully transferable until some vesting event(s) occurs, including use in executive compensation.
Restricted Stock Options	Stock options that were not taxed until the options were sold and then taxed at the capital gains rate. Created by the 1950 Revenue Act.
Risk	Exposure to loss from various sources including financial risk associated with variations from expected return.
Risk Averse	Economic construct suggesting that actors accept lower payoff to reduce volatility.
Risk Management	Strategies used by corporations to reduce volatility and risk of various kinds through hedging and other techniques.

Terms	Definitions
Risk Neutral	Decision makers are neither risk seeking nor risk averse; presumably with no preference to uncertainly associated with potential outcomes. Risk neutrality can be preferred in a diversified investment portfolio.
Risk Premium	Higher expected payoff because of additional risk, such as the higher interest rate paid in junk bonds.
Rules-based Accounting Standards	Accounting standards are based on detailed rules, presumably increasing consistency and accuracy, but increase complexity and potentially violations of economic substance.
Sarbanes-Oxley Bill	Federal legislation of 2002, designed to fix corporate problems associated with the failure of Exxon, WorldCom, and other issues, including changes to corporate governance, auditing, and securities markets.
Securities and Exchange Commission (SEC)	Federal agency created by the SEC Act of 1934 to regulate the securities markets of the United States; its mandate includes accounting and financial reporting.
Shadow Bank	Noncommercial bank financial companies that do not take in deposits but perform a multitude of banking services, such as hedge funds, mortgage companies, and private equity funds.
Special Purpose Entities	Legal entities established for a specific purpose, usually to move assets and liabilities off balance sheet; widely used by banks for securitized assets.
Speculation	Investment in relatively risky assets, often using borrowed money.
Speed Vesting (of Stock Options)	SFAS 123R required the expensing of stock options beginning in 2006; many companies advanced the vesting date, usually to 2005, to avoid expensing the options.
Spring Loading (of options)	Practice by some companies of issuing options just before some good news event that would drive up stock price.
Stagflation	Economic position where high inflation exists with poor economic growth and high unemployment.
Stealth Compensation	Compensation to CEOs and others that is not disclosed at all (or in enough detail to show actual cost), such as pensions, various perquisites, or severance pay.
Stock Appreciation Rights	SARs permit the holders to receive the increase in fair market value of stock from the grant date, either in cash or stock.
Stock Option Backdating	Issuance of stock option with the "issue date" listed at an earlier date associated with a lower stock price, allowing recipient to a higher compensation when the option is exercised.

Terms	Definitions
Stock Options	Derivatives allowing the holder to buy (call) or sell (put) a specific amount of stock at a specific price for some period of time. Stock options are often given to executives and employees as part of their compensation and generally issued on the grant date at the market price on that date.
Structured Finance	Packaging various consumer (or commercial) loans into securities, essentially functioning as a bond with the loans held as collateral.
Supplemen-tal Executive Retirement Plans (SERPs)	Retirement plans for key employees, with benefits in additional to standard retirement plans and not subject to IRS rules (or tax benefits).
Tax Avoidance	Strategies used to legally minimize tax payments by individuals and corporations.
Tax Evasion	Illegal techniques to minimize or not pay taxes.
Transaction Cost	Specific costs to complete a contractual event, including hidden and unexpected costs.
Transparency	The concept of thorough financial disclosure based on conserva-tive accounting methods, providing the details needed for user decision making.
Troubled Asset Relief Program (TARP)	Federal government bailout of the financial system based on late 2008 legislation; as implemented, the funds were used to provide capital to major ("too big to fail") banks.
VIX Index	Chicago Board Options Exchange index to measure volatility based on options stock prices on the S&P 500 index; also called the "fear index."

Notes

Chapter 1

1. Ellig (2002).
2. SEC Regulation S-K details reporting rules for SEC filings. Section 3.5.2, Item 402, covers executive compensation requirements for the 10-K.
3. The top 200 highest paid CEOs for 2012 were compiled in the New York Times, June 25, 2013. See "Executive Pay by the Numbers," www.nytimes.com/interactive/2013/06/30/business/executive-compensation-tab. Ellison was at the top. Number 200 was General Motors CEO Daniel Akerson, making a not-so-paltry $11.1 million.
4. "GMI Ratings 2013 CEO Pay Survey Reveals CEO Pay is Still on the Rise" (2013).
5. See, for example, Jensen and Meckling (1976); Murphy (2012); and Pepper and Gore (2012).
6. Jensen and Murphy (1990a); Jensen and Murphy (1990b).
7. Baker (1938).

Chapter 2

1. Milkovich, Newman, and Gerhart (2014), p. 13.
2. Milkovich, Newman, and Gerhart (2014), pp. 9–11.
3. The Fair Labor Standards Act of 1938 was part of President Roosevelt's "Second New Deal." It established a minimum wage, maximum 44 hour work week, and guaranteed "time-and-a-half" overtime pay (initially $0.25 an hour). The Act has been amended multiple times.
4. Jensen and Murphy (1990a), p. 138.
5. Balsam (2002), p. 62. Balsam has an additional table of other executives foregoing a salary for stock options around the same time.
6. DePillis (2013).
7. AFL-CIO (2014).
8. The AFLCIO also compared relative wealth. The richest 1 percent held 35.4 percent of America's wealth, averaging over $16 million each, while the bottom 60 percent owned 1.7 percent at $13,000 each.
9. Dill (2013).
10. Dill (2013).
11. Milkovich, Newman, and Gerhart (2014), p. 45.
12. Lubin (2014).

Chapter 3

1. Prior to the creation of the SEC, executive compensation (and most other financial information) was considered proprietary and seldom publicly available. Specific accounting entries made were up to the judgment of the accountants. The SEC began requiring compensation disclosures of public companies for the top executives in the mid-1930s. Annual disclosures have been required ever since, although the specific information demanded has changed over time (usually to provide more information on more executives).

2. The Social Security Act of 1935 created Social Security, which started as a 1 percent payroll tax for both employees and employers on the first $3,000. Medicare was added in 1965 as a separate tax, initially 0.35 percent on the first $6,600 (the limit was eliminated in 1994).

3. The accounting numbers are based on *grant-date values* (an *ex ante* approach), using expected compensation rather than *realized compensation*. Options use Black-Scholes or similar models; restricted stock would use stock price on grant date. Realized values for options would be the exercise price and, for restricted stock, the stock price when the stock vests. Most academic empirical research is based on grant-date values.

4. Technology quickly became available to traders in the form of Texas Instruments calculators, which would calculate the options value when the variable amounts were entered. The TI-83 Plus and other calculators are still available as are several websites to calculate Black Scholes and other pricing models.

5. Murphy (2012), p. 51.

6. See Giroux (2006), pp. 92–94, for more information on heavy use of options by tech companies. HP for example had options of 18.9 percent of shares outstanding in 2004, while IBM had 15.3 percent.

7. Many books have been written about Enron and its abusive practices, including Eichenwald (2005), McLean and Elkind (2003), and Swartz and Watkins (2003).

8. Petra and Dorata (2012), p. 1.

9. There are several items that are gains and losses recorded directly to stockholders' equity as OCI rather than through net income, including certain marketable securities gains and losses, foreign currency holding gains and losses, and certain derivative items, in addition to pension and OPEB adjustments.

10. Discount rates are used to discount future obligations and then discount the future obligations back to the present value. They could be based on long-term interest rates such as Treasuries, cost of capital, and other factors.

11. Giroux (2006), p. 112.

12. Bebchuk and Jackson (2005), pp. 1–2.
13. When I conduct a financial analysis of a corporation, I usually consider an underfunded pension plan a concern and a large negative amount a red flag.
14. U.S. Securities and Exchange Commission (n.d.).

Chapter 4

1. Frydman and Saks (2010), p. 2131.
3. Murphy (2011).
4. According to Giroux (2013, vol. 2, p. 446): "The Pecora Commission (1932–4) was a Senate investigation of the causes of the Crash of 1929, named for the last chief counsel, Ferdinand Pecora. After the crash, the economy went into depression and thousands of banks failed. Pecora uncovered many unscrupulous financial practices that shocked the nation and led to several reform bills that included the creation of the Securities and Exchange Commission."
5. Baker (1938), p. 251.
6. Baker (1938), p. 261.
7. Two companies, Woolworth and Kresge, paid commissions to executives rather than a salary. Only four companies used stock options. Marshall Field and Montgomery Ward each gave options on 100,000 shares to hire outside executives (Baker 1938, 196).
8. Baker (1938), p. 236.
9. Baker (1938), p. 208.
10. Securities and Exchange Commission (undated), *The Laws That Govern the Securities Industry*, www.sec.gov/about/laws.shtml.
11. Form 10-K was created by the SEC as the required annual financial accounting report to be submitted to the SEC under the 1934 Act. In 1935, the 10-K required corporations to disclose the total compensation (base pay plus cash and stock bonuses and stock options) of the three top executives making over $20,000 a year. In 1938, the SEC required executive compensation (still the top three) to be disclosed in the annual proxy statement.
12. *The New Republic* apparently was the first to compare the executive compensation to the average salary of workers within the industry: "In 1936, for instance, a reader could compare the annual salary of Jones & Laughlin Steel's president—$250,000—to the average weekly wage of a steelworker—$17" (Wells 2011, 9).
13. The term *Great Compression* was coined in a 1992 economics article by Claudia Goldin and Robert Margo for "the narrowing of the wage structure in the 1940s … and were regarded as 'just' even after the egalitarian pressures of World War II had disappeared" (Goldin and Margo 1992, 2–3).

14. Sloan (1963), p. 377.

15. The "Treaty of Detroit" was a bargain between General Motors and the United Auto Workers (UAW) giving UAW workers salaries rising with productivity plus health and retirement benefits. This became a model for other manufacturers in the auto industry and beyond. Autos and other heavy manufacturing industries stayed reasonably accommodating to labor until foreign competition and other factors in the 1970s made them uncompetitive.

16. An important characteristic of the issuance of options to executives and employees is that the holder participates in corporate success (based on stock price) with no risk associated with stock price declines (unlike stockholders)—that is, "underwater options" would not be exercised. This may encourage executives to take greater risks than preferred by stockholders.

17. The 1954 Revenue Act made two changes. It limited the exercise term to 10 years (which is still the most common term limit) and allowed option repricing (to lower levels) if the stock price of previously granted options declined after the original grant date.

18. Frydman and Saks (2010), p. 2108.

19. Specific terms included:

    Executives were required to hold stock acquired through option exercises for three years (rather than six months) in order to be taxed at the lower capital gains rate. Exercise prices were to be set at no less than 100 percent of the grant-date market prices. The maximum option term was reduced from ten years to five years. The option price could not be reduced during the term of the option, nor could an option be exercised while there was an outstanding option issued to the executive at an earlier time (Murphy 2011, 12).

20. The previous secular bear market was from the Great Depression of the early 1930s to the end of the Korean War in the early 1950.

21. "The Great Divergence" was chapter 7 of Krugman's 2007 book *The Conscience of a Liberal.*

22. Hall and Liebrum (2003).

23. See Murphy (2012), pp. 75–78.

24. Murphy (2012), pp. 72–73.

25. Levitt and Dwyer (2002), p. 107.

26. Also in the early 1990s, the SEC wanted public corporations to disclose the value of options (based on a pricing model) in the Proxy Statement's Summary Compensation Table to require corporations to correctly value total compensation by the major executives. After fierce lobbying, the SEC backed off and required companies to include only the number of options rather than the value.

27. The impact of SFAS No. 123 proved quite remarkable, especially for high-tech companies. In an earlier book, I showed the use of options by four blue chip tech companies for 2003 (Giroux 2006, 93):

Company	Options outstanding (million)	Options to shares outstanding (%)
Microsoft	949	8.8
Hewlett-Packard	550	18.9
Intel	884	14.1
IBM	252	15.3

Options to shares represent potential dilution. For the 30 companies of the DOW, it averaged 9 percent. The real costs of options during this period were substantial, but essentially ignored.

28. Murphy (2012), pp. 86–88. Over the period 1992 to 2005, the S&P 500 companies paid out options worth $800 billion, equivalent to 25 percent of outstanding shares.

29. Giroux (2008), p. 1226.

30. Murphy (2012), pp. 87, 97.

31. Another factor is that stock options are more popular in a bull market as greater returns are expected and not in a bear market. A substantial market downturn occurred during the Great Recession.

32. An interesting case was seen in 2014 when Berkshire Hathaway CEO Warren Buffett called Coca-Cola's executive pay plan "excessive" (Berkshire is Coca-Cola's largest stockholder). However, Berkshire abstained from voting the shares on this issue, with Buffett claiming that taking them on was "like belching at the dinner table. You can't do it too often."

33. GMI Ratings 2013 Pay Survey reported that Zuckerberg received $2.3 billion and Kinder $1.1 billion, while the top 10 each received over $100 million in total compensation. Median compensation for the S&P 500 was up almost 20 percent. GMI Ratings were based on surveys of over 2,200 public companies (www3.gmiratings.com/home/2013/10/).

Chapter 5

1. Agency theory was initially based on the *law of agency*, a legal term about contractual (and other) fiduciary relationships, where the principal authorizes the agent to create legal relationships with third parties. The internal relationship is called principal agent; the agents have external relationships with the third parties plus the relationship between the principal and the third party (based on the common law principal that acting through others is the same as acting directing with oneself).

2. Adam Smith identified the potential conflicts between big corporations and hired executives, the analysis of which was expanded by Berle and Means (1932) and others. Berle and Means stated the premise of "managerialism" as: "The separation of ownership from control produces a condition where the interests of owner and of ultimate manager may, and often do, diverge, and where many of the checks which formerly operated to limit the use of power disappear" (Berle and Means 1932, 25).

3. Hundreds of executive compensation articles exist. This short analysis attempts to focus on those that are particularly important, including a number of surveys that each explore many more studies, usually from a specific perspective. Analysis of academic articles from foreign countries and the United States to international comparisons is presented in Chapter 6.

4. Jensen and Meckling (1976), p. 308.

5. Jensen and Meckling (1976), p. 308.

6. A special case exists when a government bailout is expected. For example, one reason that investment banks and other large financial institutions were willing to take extraordinary risks in the subprime meltdown of 2008 was the likelihood of a Federal Reserve/Treasury bailout because of the *too big to fail* principle.

7. Jensen and Murphy (1990b). However, other factors should also be used in an optimal contract to better evaluate the CEOs' *unobservable choice of action*, such as accounting measures of performance (Jensen and Murphy 1990b, 245).

8. Missing data resulted in 1,699 CEOs from 1,049 corporations representing 7,750 CEO-years of changes in compensation. Stock option data were not available; consequently, options-based analysis was based on 73 Fortune 500 manufacturing firms from 1969 through 1983. Data related to poor performance and CEO terminations were limited. CEO total wealth (to calculate *wealth at risk*) could not be determined. Finally, a sample of large NYSE companies (upper quartile) of the 1930 was compared to a similar sample of NYSE firms from the upper quartile from the 1974 to 1986 period.

9. Once again, relevant data were difficult to get and interpret. The average CEO served about 10 years, making it difficult to determine whether he or she retired rather than being fired for cause. Most of the terminations were for CEOs (60 percent) between 60 and 66 years of age.

10. Jensen and Murphy (1990b, 257). In my interpretation of the Jensen/Murphy empirical data, the CEOs had performance-based pay as part of their earnings portfolios and therefore not *paid like bureaucrats*. Presumably, the amount of performance-based pay was insufficient according to Jensen and Murphy.

11. Murphy (2012), pp. 72–73.

12. It was not just CEOs who received options. Some 95 percent of the options granted were to lower-level executives and employees. The option explosion was especially true for high-tech companies and start-ups. Because the granting of options did not result in a compensation expense at the time, companies could compensate for low pay by issuing options. Low-level employees at successful companies (say a Google) could become millionaires and the founders, billionaires. Unfortunately, many failed and the option holdings became worthless.

13. As seen in earlier periods for movements away from cash salary, the explosion was on top of other types of compensation. That is, salary, cash bonuses, and so on did not go down. The options explosion and failures to reduce other forms of compensation are difficult to explain theoretically. Because options are inefficient as a form of short-term compensation, it is even more difficult to theoretically explain the wide use of options for lower-level employees.

14. Murphy (2012), p. 142.

15. See Murphy and Zabojnik (2007); Frydman (2007).

16. See Gabaix and Landier (2008).

17. Yermack (1997).

18. Yermack (2009).

19. Hartzell, Ofek, and Yermack (2004).

20. Yermack (2006b).

21. Yermack (2006a).

22. Murphy (2012), p. 138.

23. Jensen and Murphy (1990b).

24. Yermack (1997).

25. Yermack (1997), p. 449.

26. Hall and Liebman (1998).

27. Hall and Liebman (1998), p. 686.

28. Hall and Murphy (2003).

29. Options do not provide efficient incentives to lower-level employees and free rider problems exist. More efficient pay-performance incentives include bonuses and other cash-based plans (Hall and Murphy 2003, 58).

30. The income statement and bottom line numbers such as net income are based on accounting standards rather than *real* or *economic income*. According to most economics-based literature, investors see through the *veil of accounting*, but real-world considerations make analysis difficult.

31. Hall and Murphy (2003), p. 69.

32. Murphy and Zabojnik (2007).

33. Frydman and Jetner (2010.

34. Frydman and Saks (2010).

35. Piketty and Saez (2003).

36. Stock repurchases are *stock friendly*, showing corporate support for their ongoing stock price. (The decrease in equity and the artificial nature of the impact on stock price are usually downplayed.) Dividends increase total stockholder returns but not share-price appreciation. See Hall and Murphy (2003, 60).
37. Jensen and Murphy (1990a, 1990b).
38. Tosi et al. (2000), p. 301.
39. Tosi et al. (2000).
40. Efendi, Srivastava, and Swanson (2007).
41. Financial (or earnings) restatements are revised financial information that was reported previously (usually in an earlier annual report), often used as an indicator of financial manipulation or fraud.
42. Calculated as the number of options held times the excess of the stock price over the exercise price (Efendi Srivastava, and Swanson 2007).
43. Armstrong, Jagolinzer, and Larcker (2010).
44. Armstrong, Jagolinzer, and Larcker (2010), p. 236.
45. Armstrong , Jagolinzer, and Larcker (2010), p. 251.
46. Hall and Murphy (2003), p. 51.
47. Yermack (1997).
48. Lie (2005). See especially his Figure 1 (p. 807) that demonstrates the grant date as the date with the most negative cumulative abnormal returns.
49. Murphy and Sandino (2010), p. 248.
50. Murphy and Sandino (2010).
51. Murphy and Sandino also noted the similarities of compensation consultant conflicts to auditor independence and financial analyst conflicts (2010, p. 261).
52. See Murphy (2012), especially p. 97, and Figure 4.4 in Chapter 4 of this book.
53. Murphy (2012), p. 97.
54. Brookman and Thistle (2013).
55. Brookman and Thistle (2013).
56. Pepper and Gore (2012). Their model of agency theory changes various agency theory assumptions such as assuming agents are *boundedly rational* and there are extrinsic motivations for managers beyond pecuniary awards.
57. Larkin, Pierce, and Gino (2012), p. 1195.
58. Pepper and Gore (2012).
59. Mishima et al. (2010).
60. Baker and Wurgler (2011).
61. Baker and Wurgler (2011), pp. 50–80.
62. Rebitzer and Taylor (2011).
63. See Rebitzer and Taylor (2011).

Chapter 6

1. Fernandes et al.(2013).
2. Considerable variation existed across countries, with mean pay from $1.6 million in Belgium to $6.1 million in Switzerland—actually higher than in the United States. See Fernandes et al. (2013), p. 328.
3. Fernandes et al. (2013).
4. Corporations that want to list their stock on U.S. exchanges must reconcile their financial statements to U.S. GAAP. Some have asked the question about the legality of the SEC or FASB transferring responsibility for financial reporting to a non-U.S. entity such as the IASB. To the best of my knowledge, this has not been resolved. However, the SEC shows no signs of giving up GAAP responsibility.
5. The standards vary from issue to issue, but many U.S. standards follow detailed and fairly rigid rules, irrespective of economic substance (such as leases). In the case of leases, cottage industries developed to provide firms with operating leases for accounting purposes (and not reported on the balance sheet), even though for practical purposes they were capital leases. Principles-based requirements, at least in theory, focus on economic substance and provide fewer detailed rules.
6. The European Union was formally established by the Maastricht Treaty of 1993, building on the earlier European Coal and Steel Community and European Economic Community of the 1950s. The economic integration of Europe continues.
7. Institutional and agency theories are not mutually exclusive and institutional factors (such as specific formal institutions) can be used as moderators or control variables. See, for example, Van Essen et al. (2012), pp. 399–402.
8. This was also the first real comparison of actual compensation possible between the United States and any European country. Canada also provided individual top executive pay, while a number of countries required aggregate pay for top executives as a group but did not disclose individual pay.
9. Conyon and Murphy (2000).
10. Disney's CEO Michael Eisner topped the U.S. list at an amazing $574 million (thanks to exercising accumulated options), while Britain's highest paid CEO, Sam Chisolm of British Sky Broadcasting, made a relatively paltry $11.2 million.Conyon and Murphy (2000) state numbers in £, which are restated to dollars at a rate of $1.65 to a £ (the average exchange rate in 1997).
11. Conyon and Murphy (2000), p. F667.
12. Zhou (2000).
13. Compensation was based on the 1993-5 averages using 1991 Canadian dollars (Zhou 2000, 219).

14. Conyon and Schwalback (2000).

15. "The pay variable for the UK is the salary and bonus of the highest paid director and excludes stock options and other long-term elements of pay. For Germany, the pay measure is the per capital income of the main board" (Conyon and Schwalbach 2000, 512).

16. Similar data limitations mainly using the Towers Perrin (now Towers Watson, a consulting firm) surveys are true of most early studies, that is, before corporations across Europe and beyond were required to disclose executive compensation data on specific top executives. Towers Perrin calculated pay estimates based on questionnaires.

17. See Conyon et al. (2011), pp. 31–38, for more information on the various pay scandals and European response.

18. See Conyon et al. (2011), pp. 36–39 and Fernandes et al. (2013), pp. 327–28.

19. Fernandes et al. (2013).

20. The imputed pay premium varies from 0 percent to 18 percent depending on the specific model used, although statistically insignificant in each case. See Fernandes et al. (2013), pp. 339–46.

21. Fernandes et al. (2013).

22. See, especially, Fernandes et al. (2013), Table 8, p. 355.

23. Conyon et al. (2011).

24. Van Essen et al. (2012).

25. Van Essen et al. (2012), p. 413.

Chapter 7

1. Giroux (2014), pp. 17–23.

2. Strine (2012), p. 2.

3. Strine (2012), p. 2.

4. Faulkender et al. (2010), p. 115.

5. The Business Roundtable in an organization of CEOs of major U.S. corporations promoting pro-business policies. Its webpage (businessroundtable.org) lists a number of topics related to social issues, such as education, environment, and health.

6. Brooks (2013).

7. Jensen (2010), on the other hand, points out that the multi-mission structure of social responsibility (his focus is on the related concept of stakeholder theory) cannot be solved with a single-valued objective function (traditional economics attempts to maximize profits).

8. See Bebchuk and Fried (2010), especially pp. 100–102, for a discussion of this issue.

References

AFL-CIO. 2014. *Executive Pay Watch 2014.* www.aflcio.org/corporate-watch/ceopaywatch-2014.

Armstrong, C., A. Jagolinzer, and D. Larcker. 2010. "Chief Executive Officer Equity Incentives and Accounting Irregularities." *Journal of Accounting Research* 48, no. 2, pp. 225–71.

Baker, J. 1938. *Executive Salaries and Bonus Plans.* New York: McGraw-Hill Book Company.

Baker, M., and J. Wurgler. 2011. "Behavioral Corporate Finance: An Updated Survey." NBER Working Paper 17333, Cambridge: National Bureau of Economic Research.

Balsam, S. 2002. *An Introduction to Executive Compensation.* San Diego, CA: Academic Press.

Bebchuk, L., and J. Fried. 2010. "How to Tie Equity Compensation to Long-Term Results." *Journal of Applied Corporate Finance* 22, no. 1, pp. 99–106.

Bebchuk, L., and R. Jackson. 2005. "Executive Pensions." NBER Working Paper No. 11907, Cambridge, MA: National Bureau of Economic Research.

Berle, A., and G. Means. 1932. *The Modern Corporation and Private Property.* New York: Macmillan Publishing Co.

Brookman, J., and P. Thistle. 2013. "Managerial Compensation: Luck, Skill or Labor Markets?" *Journal of Corporate Finance* 21, pp. 252–68.

Brooks, C. 2013. "Social Responsibility No Longer Optional for Businesses." *Business News Daily*, May 22. www.businessnewsdaily.com/4528-social-responsibility-not-optional.html.

Conyon, M., N. Fernandes, M. Ferreira, P. Matos, and K. Murphy. 2011. "The Executive Compensation Controversy: A Transatlantic Analysis." Working paper, Wharton School, University of Pennsylvania.

Conyon, M., and K. Murphy. 2000. "The Prince and the Pauper? CEO Pay in the United States and United Kingdom." *The Economic Journal* 110, no. 467, pp. F640–71.

Conyon, M., and J. Schwalbach. 2000. "Executive Compensation: Evidence from the UK and Germany." *Long-range Planning* 33, no. 4, pp. 504–26.

DePillis, L. 2013. "Why is the U.S.'s 1 Percent So Much Richer Than Everyone Else?" http://www.washingtonpost.com/blogs/wonkblog/wp/2013/08/09/why-is-the-u-s-s-1-percent-so-much-richer-than-everywhere-else/?tid=rssfeed

Dill, K. 2013. "CEO Pay Has Risen More Than Twice as Much as the Stock Market." *Forbes*, June 27. www.forbes.com/sites/kathryndill/2013/06/27, (accessed June 6).

Efendi, J., A. Srivastava, and E. Swanson. 2007. "Why Do Corporate Managers Misstate Financial Statements? The Role of Option Compensation and Other Factors." *Journal of Financial Economy* 85, no. 3, pp. 667–708.

Eichenwald, K. 2005. *Conspiracy of Fools*. New York, NY: Broadway Books.

Ellig, B. 2002. *The Complete Guide to Executive Compensation*. New York: McGraw-Hill.

Faulkender, M., D. Kayyrzhanova, N. Prabhala, and L. Senbet. 2010. "Executive Compensation: An Overview of Research on Corporate Practices and Proposed Reforms." *Journal of Applied Corporate Finance* 22, no. 1, pp. 107–18.

Fernandes, N., M. Ferreira, P. Matos, and K. Murphy. 2013. "Are U.S. CEOs Paid More? New International Evidence." *The Review of Financial Studies* 26, no. 2, pp. 323–67.

Frydman, C. 2007. "Rising Through the Ranks: The Evolution of the Market for Corporate Executives, 1936–2003." Working Paper, Cambridge: Harvard University Working Paper.

Frydman, C., and D. Jenter. 2010. "CEO Compensation." *Annual Review of Financial Economics* 2, no. 1, pp. 75–102.

Frydman, C., and R. Saks. 2010. "Executive Compensation: A New View from a Long-term Perspective, 1936–2005." *The Review of Financial Studies* 23, no. 5, pp. 2099–138.

Gabaix, X., and A. Landier. 2008. "Why Has CEO Pay Increased So Much?" *Quarterly Journal of Economics*, 123, pp. 49–100.

Giroux, G. 2006. *Earnings Magic and the Unbalance Sheet: The Search for Financial Reality*. New York: John Wiley & Sons.

Giroux, G. 2008. "What Went Wrong? Accounting Fraud and Lessons from Recent Scandals." *Social Research: An International Quarterly of the Social Sciences* 75, no. 4, pp. 1205–38.

Giroux, G. 2013. *Business Scandals, Corruption, and Reform, an Encyclopedia*. Santa Barbara, CA: Greenwood.

Giroux, G. 2014. *Accounting Fraud: Maneuvering and Manipulation, Past and Present*. New York: Business Expert Press.

"GMI Ratings 2013. CEO Pay Survey Reveals CEO Pay is Still on the Rise." October 22, 2013. *GMI Ratings*. www3.gmiratings.com/home/2013/10

Goldin, C., and R. Margo. February 1992. "The Great Compression: The Wage Structure in the United States at Mid-Century." *The Quarterly Journal of Economics* 107, no. 1, pp. 1–34.

Hall, B., and J. Liebman.1998. "Are CEOs Really Paid Like Bureaucrats?" *Quarterly Journal of Economics* 113, no. 3, pp. 653–91.

Hall, B., and K. Murphy. 2003."The Trouble with Stock Options." *Journal of Economic Perspectives* 17, no. 3, pp. 49–70.

Hartzell, J., E. Ofek, and D. Yermack. 2004. "What's in it for Me? CEOs Whose Firms Are Acquired." *Review of Financial Studies* 17, no. 1, pp. 37–61.

Jensen, M. 2010. "Value Maximization, Stakeholder Theory, and the Corporate Objective Function." *Journal of Applied Corporate Finance* 22, no. 1, pp. 32–42.

Jensen, M., and W. Meckling. 1976. "Theory of the Firm: Managerial Behavior, Agency Costs and Ownership Structure." *Journal of Financial Economics* 3, pp. 305–60.

Jensen, M., and K. Murphy. May–June 1990a. "CEO Incentives—It's Not How Much You Pay, But How." *Harvard Business Review*, pp. 138–49.

Jensen, M., and K. Murphy. April 1990b. "Performance Pay and Top-Management Incentives." *Journal of Political Economy* 98, no. 2, pp. 225–64.

Larkin, I., L. Pierce, and F. Gino. 2012. "The Psychological Costs of Pay-for-Performance: Implications for the Strategic Compensation of Employees." *Strategic Management Journal* 33, pp. 1194–1214.

Levitt, A., and P. Dwyer. 2002. *Take on the Street: What Wall Street and Corporate America Don't Want you to Know.* New York: Pantheon Books.

Lie, E. 2005. "On the Timing of CEO Stock Option Awards." *Management Science* 51, no. 5, pp. 802–12.

Lubin, J. April 15, 2014. "GE Rethinks the 20-Year CEO." *Wall Street Journal*, April 15. *online.wsj.com/news/articles/SB10001424052702304572204579501640452285598.*

McLean, B., and P. Elkind. 2003. *The Smartest Guys in the Room: The Amazing Rise and Scandalous Fall of Enron.* New York: Portfolio/Penguin.

Milkovich, G., J. Newman, and B. Gerhart. 2014. *Compensation, Eleventh Edition.* New York: McGraw-Hill.

Mishima, Y., B. Dykes, E. Block, and T. Pollock. 2010. "Why 'Good' Firms Do Bad Things: The Effect of High Aspirations, High Expectations, and Prominence on the Incidence of Corporate Illegality." *Academy of Management Journal* 53, no. 4, pp. 701–722.

Murphy, K. 2011. "The Politics of Pay: A Legislative History of Executive Compensation." Marshall Research Paper Series Working Paper FBE 01.11.

Murphy, K. 2012. "Executive Compensation: Where We Are, and How We Got Here." Working Paper, Los Angeles, CA: University of Southern California.

Murphy, K., and T. Sandino. 2010. "Executive Pay and 'Independent' Compensation Consultants." *Journal of Accounting and Economics* 49, no. 3, pp. 247–62.

Murphy, K., and J. Zabojnik. 2007. "Managerial Capital and the Market for CEOs." *Social Science Research Network.* papers.ssrn.com/sol3/papers.cfm?abstract_id=984376.

Pepper, A., and J. Gore. 2012. "Behavioral Agency Theory: New Foundation for Theorizing about Executive Compensation." *Journal of Management.* http://jom.sagepub.com/content/early/2012/09/26/0149206312461054.abstract

Petra, S., and N. Dorata. 2012. "Restricted Stock Awards and Taxes: What Employees and Employers Should Know." *Journal of Accountancy* 213, no. 2, pp. 44–48.

Piketty, T. 2014. *Capital in the Twenty-First Century*. Cambridge, MA: The Belknap Press of Harvard University Press.

Piketty, T., and E. Saez. February 2003. "Income Inequality in the United States, 1913–1998." *Quarterly Journal of Economics* 118, no.1, pp. 1–40.

Rebitzer, J., and L Taylor. 2011. "Extrinsic Rewards and Intrinsic Motives: Standard and Behavioral Approaches to Agency and Labor Markets." In *Handbook of Labor Economics, Volume 4A*, eds. D. Card, and O. Ashenfelter. New York: Elsevier.

Sloan, A. 1963. *My Years with General Motors*. New York: Doubleday.

Strine, L. 2012. "Our Continuing Struggle with the Idea That For-profit Corporations Seek Profit." *Wake Forest Law Review* 47, no. 1, www.wakeforest lawreview.com.

Swartz, M., and S. Watkins. 2003. *Power Failure: The Inside Story of the Collapse of Enron*. New York: Doubleday.

Tosi, H., S. Werner, J. Katz, and L. Gomez-Mejia. 2000. "How Much Does Performance Matter? A Meta-Analysis of CEO Pay Studies." *Journal of Management* 26, no. 2, pp. 301–39.

U.S. Securities and Exchange Commission. n.d. "Executive Compensation." www.sec.gov/answeres/execomp.htm

Van Essen, M., P. Heugens, J. Otten, and J. Van Oosterhout. 2012. "An Institution-based View of Executive Compensation: A Multilevel Meta-analytic Test." *Journal of International Business Studies* 43, pp. 396–23.

Wells, H. 2011. "U.S. Executive Compensation in Historical Perspective." *Temple Legal Research Paper Series, Research Paper No. 2011-19*.

Yermack, D. 1997. "Good Timing: CEO Stock Option Awards and Company News Announcements." *Journal of Finance* 52, no. 2, pp. 449–76.

Yermack, D. 2006a. "Flights of Fancy: Corporate Jets, CEO Perquisites, and Inferior Shareholder Returns." *Journal of Financial Economics* 80, no. 1, pp. 211–42.

Yermack, D. 2006ab. "Golden Handshakes: Separation Pay for Retired and Dismissed CEOs." *Journal of Accounting and Economics* 41, no. 3, pp. 237–56.

Yermack, D. 2009. "Deductio Ad Absurdum: CEOs Donating Their Own Stock to Their Own Family Foundations." *Journal of Financial Economics* 94, no. 1, pp. 107–23.

Zhou, X. 2000. "CEO Pay, Firm Size, and Corporate Performance: Evidence from Canada," *Canadian Journal of Economics* 33, no. 1, pp. 213–51.

Index

www.ingramcontent.com/pod-product-compliance
Lightning Source LLC
Chambersburg PA
CBHW072307210326
41519CB00057B/3047